Country Roads
~ of ~
CONNECTICUT
and
RHODE ISLAND

*A Guide Book
from Country Roads Press*

Country Roads
~ of ~
# CONNECTICUT
and
RHODE ISLAND

Steve Sherman

Illustrated by
Victoria Sheridan

Country Roads Press
CASTINE · MAINE

Country Roads of Connecticut and Rhode Island
© 1994 by Steve Sherman. All rights reserved.

Published by Country Roads Press
P.O. Box 286, Lower Main Street
Castine, Maine 04421

Text and cover design by Edith Allard.
Illustrations by Victoria Sheridan.

ISBN 1-56626-037-X

Library of Congress Cataloging-in-Publication Data

Sherman, Steve, 1938–
     Country roads of Connecticut and Rhode Island / by Steve Sherman ;
   illustrated by Victoria Sheridan.
          p.   cm.
     Includes index.
     ISBN 1-56626-037-X : $9.95
     1. Connecticut—Tours.   2. Rhode Island—Tours.   3. Automobile
   travel—Connecticut—Guidebooks.   4. Automobile travel—Rhode
   Island—Guidebooks.   I. Title.
   F92.3.S54   1994
   917.4504′43—dc20   93-30335
                                                                  CIP

Printed in the United States of America.
10 9 8 7 6 5 4 3 2 1

*Would that all days could be spent on back roads
talking to strangers and staring at the rose
sandcastle of a church, watching a gardener pick a rose,
throat and brow patterned by the warm rose
light in the sculptured shadows of back roads.*

*—from "Sunday on the Green"
by Julia Older*

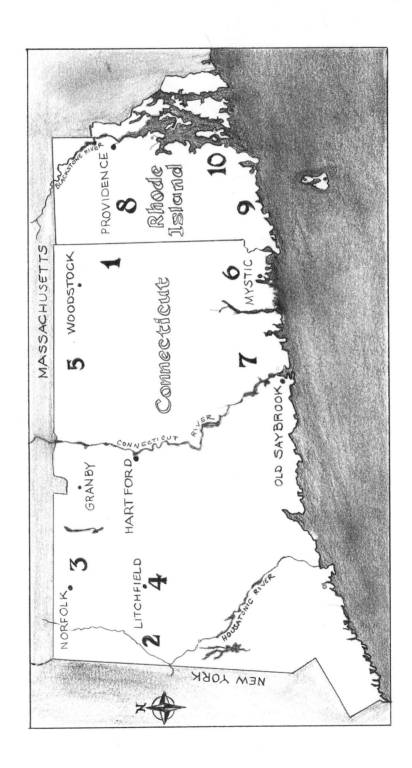

Contents

(& Key to Country Roads of Connecticut and Rhode Island)

Introduction

Connecticut and Rhode Island, two of the smallest states in the Union, offer some of the biggest opportunities for enjoyable country driving. Although it is ranked as the fiftieth state in size at scarcely more than one thousand square miles, Rhode Island sports twenty-eight state parks and forests, scores of inviting lilliputian villages, and endlessly intriguing Narragansett Bay, which indents the state for thirty miles. Connecticut, as the third smallest state, is more than four times larger than its wee neighbor, but like Rhode Island it encompasses a surprising variety of places to prospect: the long, calm Connecticut River valley dissecting the state in half, the peaceful northwestern corner along the Housatonic River, the 250-mile shoreline of Long Island Sound to the south, the quiet corner of the northeastern side of the state, and 119 state parks and forests.

People from Rhode Island are called Rhode Islanders. But what do you call people from Connecticut? In *Smithsonian* magazine, Paul Dickson credits professor Allen Walker Read of Columbia University with deep research on this very dilemma. Professor Read found all sorts of configurations, starting in 1702 with Cotton Mather, that called people from Connecticut Connecticotians. Other attempts included Conneciticutesian, Connecticutter, Connecticutian, Connecticutile, not to mention Connecticutey, Connecticanuck, Connectikook, Connectecotton, Connecticutist, Connecticutler, and Connecticutlet. Maybe the best of all is from Allan

Pratt of New Haven, who describes those hailing from Connecticut as "Commuters."

Whatever the choice, one of the most overlooked points about both Connecticut and Rhode Island is that their cityless sections contain wonderful territory and sites to explore despite the fact that both states are highly industrialized. Rhode Island, in fact, is the second most densely populated state after New Jersey. And at least 90 percent of the three million residents in Connecticut live in metropolitan areas. Good. This leaves the rural lands, lakes, and leisurely driving to those of us who like cruising the uncluttered countryside to sample the simple and natural life.

The pleasure of these ten trips in *Country Roads of Connecticut and Rhode Island* starts with discovery. One trip takes you to fantasylike Gillette Castle State Park on the high edge of the great Connecticut River. Another excursion introduces you to the heartwarming story of a recently built wooden bridge so that little Rhode Island could lay claim to having at least one scenic covered bridge again. Another trip ends at historic Stonington village and the lighthouse point where in 1814 hardly more than a handful of stalwart new Americans repulsed a two-day naval invasion of snap-to British sailors. You'll come away remembering Roseland Cottage, the Tomaquag Indian Museum, the still-operating factory of the famous Hitchcock chair, huge Litchfield green, the secret coves and shoreline of both Rhode Island and Connecticut.

Country Roads of Connecticut and Rhode Island is intended to point the way and paint the scene. Please use it as scout and guide, route planner and reading companion. Open the pages. Enjoy the open road.

To simplify road designations, I've used the following abbreviations: I = Interstate; US = U.S. Route or Highway; State = State Route or Highway; County = County Route or Road.

CONNECTICUT

1 ~

North Woodstock to Voluntown

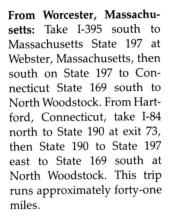

From Worcester, Massachusetts: Take I-395 south to Massachusetts State 197 at Webster, Massachusetts, then south on State 197 to Connecticut State 169 south to North Woodstock. From Hartford, Connecticut, take I-84 north to State 190 at exit 73, then State 190 to State 197 east to State 169 south at North Woodstock. This trip runs approximately forty-one miles.

Highlights: Roseland Cottage, country inns, dairy and egg farms, Pomfret School, nation's oldest agricultural fair, cider and vegetable stands, antique shops, museums, Pachaug State Forest.

North Woodstock to Pomfret

Known as the "Quiet Corner," the northeastern section of Connecticut offers some of the most pleasant towns and countrysides you'll encounter. On one hand, the state prospers under a reputation for its highly industrialized centers where 90 percent of the population lives in and around cities, especially on the southern and western stretches. Not for lack of good reason does Connecticut suffer the occasional indignity of being dismissed as a suburb of Manhattan. On the other hand, this trip far from the blare and tear of urban unction shows the Connecticut rural side, too.

3

The first half of this excursion follows State 169 through well-mannered towns and many appealing sites. Head south on State 169 at the junction of State 197 in the center of North Woodstock, a close-knit community that augurs well for the beginning of the leisurely journey to come. You'll soon cross a brook and then climb easily and steadily for a mile and a half to a high lay of the land.

For the next mile and a half you'll cruise past the Maplecrest Farm with its old and new silos, leafy cornfields and tailored orchards, cider and maple-syrup stands by the roadside. The two-lane road arches now and then over the low-lying hills in this see-for-yourself reminder that Connecticut still enjoys its agricultural past along with selling insurance and manufacturing atomic submarines.

Once you pass North Running Brook and drive up a modest incline into Woodstock, you're again on high ground at the open and attractive town center. Woodstock Academy occupies the highest of the high ground on the left. As early as 1636 Thomas Hooker led a group through this territory on his way to establishing Hartford forty miles west on a bend in the Connecticut River, which was first explored by Adrien Block in 1614. The Wabbaquessets lived in peace near here, but when King Philip's War ignited in 1675 they left the area and the fighting for better climes and times. Eleven years later a group of Europeans, the first to settle here, trekked from Roxbury in the Massachusetts Bay Colony and became known as the "Thirteen Goers." In fond memory they named their township New Roxbury (it's now Windham County). For the next three score and three years, Woodstock remained part of the Massachusetts Bay Colony until in 1749 the settlers found it more sensible to secede and join the Connecticut Colony. By 1775 it made even more sense for Captain, and later General, Samuel McClellan and his 184 men to join the shots heard 'round the world at Lexington and Concord and secede from the whole British Empire.

Woodstock's rosy pink Roseland Cottage

Directly opposite Woodstock Academy the pink-painted Roseland Cottage stands as a preeminent eye-catcher. This carpenter Gothic Revival of 1846 decorative gingerbread façade was built as a summer home for Henry C. Bowen, publisher and host to Presidents Grant, Hayes, Harrison, and McKinley. Bowen founded the *Independent*, a courageous, vanguard pre–Civil War newspaper that crusaded against slavery. You'll enjoy the summer tours inside and out of this showcase cottage mansion complete with original furnishings, ice house, aviary, and indoor bowling alley.

Continue slowly through the town center, past the 1690 First Congregational Church that dominates a slight rise in the town center, and the well-kept houses spaced comfortably in the openness of this winsome town. After passing Woodstock Orchards and Harold Bishop's sweet cider and apples for sale on the right in late summer and early fall, the Inn at Woodstock Hill on the right overlooks a long slant of the land and horizon. The old estate on fourteen acres now offers nineteen suites and guest rooms that combine an upscale attention to detail and pink-cloth fine dining with four-poster country charm, "where the world is the way it's meant to be."

Three-quarters of a mile out of town, continue south on State 169 as it veers downhill slightly to the right from the junction of State 171. Two-tenths of a mile later, on the right among a small gathering of small businesses, the Fox Hunt Farms Gourmet Shop might coincide with your schedule for a good food break. Inside the rustic front await all sorts of delights: European-style raspberry-filled croissants, twenty varieties of coffee, choice cheeses galore, sandwiches and salads, select ice creams, breads and brioche, and "Famous Fudge Made on Premises."

If these taste-bud temptations don't beckon you, maybe the establishment's rhymes will:

A scenic stop at the country shop
Brings delight with every bite.

Breads are baking
Coffee is brewing.
Over 50 cheeses
You'll be viewing.

Plus hard-to-find gourmet treats
Fresh made fudge & other sweets.
Hear that familiar "feed me" alarm?
Get yourself to Fox Hunt Farms!

The neatly dormant Woodstock Fair Grounds diagonally across the way spring to life on Labor Day weekend in the fall when the judging, games, and festivities are held. In the meantime, remain on State 169, turning to the right after another tenth of a mile, and continue south past the old Data General Conference Center building complex, then the Woodstock Airport about a mile later, and Spruce Hill Farm on the left about another mile.

In three-tenths of a mile the Pomfret town-line sign appears, a signal to look quickly to the right through a border row of trees behind a low-lying, flat-stone wall. Through the tree trunks and branches you'll see an intriguing, handsome stone barn and house of precision construction.

A little less than a mile and a half later, a stop sign halts you at the junction of State 97 and US 44; stay straight ahead on State 169 south. You're now in the core of small-town Pomfret, a well-manicured center that fits its official appellation of a "Scenic Route" in this Quiet Corner of Connecticut. On the northwest corner you can't miss the Vanilla Bean Cafe, a popular sandwich, salad, and sweets restaurant. This informal, chalkboard-menu restaurant offers food prepared by an accomplished hand in a seat-yourself atmosphere. Folk-music entertainment is staged Friday and Saturday nights at eight o'clock.

Scattered here and there in the vicinity are other attractions for the eye and mind, including the intriguing Brayton Grist Mill and Marcy Blacksmith Museum with blacksmithing equipment and machinery. They're found off US 44 to the left a couple miles at the entrance to Mashamoquet Brook State Park. Sandra Lee's 2.5-acre herb and flower farm and retail shop are situated in Pomfret Center on nearby State 97. In addition, many eighteenth-century estates and farmhouses have been updated and converted into attractive inns and bed-and-breakfast accommodations.

But the centerpiece of Pomfret has to be the Pomfret School. Founded in 1894 by William E. Peck, you can't miss its long, single row of neat-and-trim brick buildings as you steer easily down State 169 through the heart of town. This college preparatory school of 300 students encompassing grades nine through twelve belongs to the heralded prep school tradition that has educated and trained many social and political leaders of the country. On 500 acres of classrooms, dormitories, and playing fields, Pomfret School sticks to Peck's original goals of equipping young men, and as of 1968 young women, to enter colleges and universities through a heavy load of academics, the arts, and sports along with a commensurate load of character training in honesty, self-discipline, service, and honor.

In keeping with the original intent, students develop their imaginative and spiritual talents with music, theater, and painting in addition to four required years of English, three years of math, three years of a modern or classical language, and the sciences, not to mention football, tennis, ice hockey, and baseball. Since this classic curriculum is administered to students of the modern world, so too do they study computer science, delve into film and photography, and play soccer, squash, and lacrosse.

So prep schools have not gone the way of the player piano, as you plainly see firsthand driving by the ivy-covered school.

Brooklyn to Canterbury

As you leave Pomfret on State 169 south, US 44 to the right leads to Mashamoquet Brook State Park a couple minutes away. The trees and picnic tables make this a handy, relaxing spot for rest and recreation (fishing, lounging, walking the forested grounds, picnicking). If you don't wish to stop, continue south on State 169 toward Brooklyn, crossing State 101 a half mile later, then the Lapsley Orchard two miles after this, where flatland apple orchards bloom pinkish white in early spring, turn full-blown green in summer, droop heavy-hung-with-red-fruit in fall. Bagfuls of fruit are for sale at the roadside stand on the left.

The Brooklyn town line shortly afterward appears before you reach the heart of this crossroads town at US 6, with a stoplight three miles later. In between these points you'll pass robust cornfields in high summer, isolated families living the quiet life, easy-to-drive terrain with secreted brooks and clusters of woodland.

At the US 6 stoplight and to your left, the Trinity Parish Stone Church stands its grounds with irrefutable panache. Then straight ahead on State 169 a half mile later the Brooklyn Fair Grounds boasts in giant letters of hosting the oldest continuous annual agricultural fair in the nation—since 1852. By then the town had been established for thirty-four years, although the area had been settled since 1703 as Mortlake, not an overly appetizing name. The fair is held in late August.

The six miles to the center of Canterbury take you past some vegetable stands and laid-back countryside. Take your time and enjoy the leisureliness that the narrow road engenders. Leave the neon signs behind. Forget the skyscrapers.

The stop sign at the small rise in the road at State 14 brings you to full-fledged Michael's Market on the right, in case you need supplies. Canterbury sank its confident roots in 1703 when the English settlers borrowed a famous name to label their town. But, of course, as the years passed the settlers became more American until the tension finally snapped in 1775. Canterbury provided its share of revolutionary warriors, including Moses Cleveland, born here in 1754. He founded Cleveland, Ohio, in 1796 on a strip of land along the shore of Lake Erie, known as the Western Reserve; Case Western Reserve University got its name from it.

During the formulating years of the nation, Connecticut Colony and Pennsylvania disputed western borderlands, a clash that in 1782 was settled in favor of Pennsylvania by the Trenton Decree. All that remained for Connecticut was the south shore-strip known as the Western Reserve. Four years later Connecticut ceded all of its western lands, except the prized Western Reserve, to the United States. In 1792 grants of these "firelands" in the Western Reserve were made to residents of nine "suffering towns" that had been damaged by British raids during the Revolution. Tracts of half a million acres were set aside for resettlement by those burned-out residents. Demographics and politics further established commonsensical proprietary rights until the obvious became overwhelming. In 1800 Connecticut relinquished all title to the Western Reserve to the United States. Curiously, General Moses Cleveland returned to his home roots of Canterbury and in 1806 died there.

Directly across State 14 from Michael's Market stands the home and boarding school of Prudence Crandall, a different kind of warrior. A Quaker, Prudence accepted young Negro girls as day students in her boarding school in 1833. The lemon yellow, two-story historic building, once operating as the first school for young Black girls in New England, is now a museum open to the public. You'll see period furnishings, a research library, and how brave Prudence "suffered prejudice and bigotry and snobbery of Puritan intolerance." She was prosecuted and convicted under the education "black law" prohibiting instruction of fugitive Blacks without the consent of local authorities. For Prudence Crandall justice was the authority. She was released later upon appeal.

Plainfield to Voluntown

At the corner of Michael's Market and Prudence Crandall's boarding school in Canterbury, take State 14 east to Plainfield for a trip that eventually winds through some fine farmland. First, you have to cross the bridge over the wide Quinebaug River in a half mile, and then be sure to steer straight ahead onto State 14A. In 2.5 miles you'll drive through a thirty-mile-per-hour residential section. Follow the left-turn sign to State 14A after a stop sign; continue on another three-quarters of a mile into the center of Plainfield, which—let's face it—lives up to its name.

As you approach a T junction and a signal light at the top of a rise, turn left again onto State 14A. In four-tenths of a mile, turn right, on State 14A still, and continue uphill. In another four-tenths of a mile, you'll drive under I-395. For the next mile climb gradually into hillside apple orchards and cornfields. This undulating road by backcountry farms, some of which seem as tired as the road beneath you, continues for another mile and a half.

When you breach the narrowness of the road at the Sterling four corners, turn right on State 49 south. Soon enough the road flattens through high land into either fallow, wide-open fields or thickens up with rich, heavy cornstalks, depending on the season that finds you here. This is the country of dairy farms, and one comes up soon. About a mile

11

later a wonderful long view to the left and east catches your eye as the land tilts toward the rolling-down horizon. Another mile later you cross the Voluntown line before moving past a small residential subdivision of farmland, a sad sign of the times. Although this ridgeline territory is mostly cleared, at one time woods covered this high country, too. The area was inhabited by the Narragansetts, Pequots, and Mohegans, but intrusions by the New Worlders created social pressures and political coalitions. By the late 1600s the Mohegans sided with the colonists against the Narragansetts and Pequots, who were losers of their homelands. In 1700 a six-mile-square tract was given to some of the early settlers and veterans of the war. The heart of this tract became Volunteers' Town, which turned into Voluntown when it was incorporated twenty years later.

In about five minutes the land slants down, and in short order farmland turns to brush, which turns to pines, which turn into a Christmas tree farm—all within a half mile or so.

Less than a mile later you approach the entrance to Pachaug State Forest on the right. Almost directly across the road is a boat launch to Beachdale Pond. Although it is a state forest and not a park, Pachaug nevertheless invites the public to enjoy its woodlands and minimal facilities. Immediately inside the entrance, for example, picnic tables and fire pits await use in front of a sheltered, long-and-narrow wetlands, with all the attendant picturesque repose and, if you're lucky, ducks and geese.

The 24,000-acre forest, the largest in the state, now covers six towns sixty-six years after the initial tract was purchased in 1928. White pine, hemlock, and coastal white cedar predominate in the woodlands that have thickened up since the area was extensive farmland. Abandoned cellar holes and stone walls built from the rocks gouged and cleared from the fields abound, as do sites for mills in this land of abundant brooks and streams.

12

Pachaug makes a pleasant end to the trip, although six-tenths of a mile farther down State 49 takes you to the stop-sign junction with State 138 (right to Jewett City about ten miles away). In the meantime, the forest sports nine water impoundments, seven lakes, thirty-five miles of marked hiking trails and unpaved roads, plus horse trails and scattered picnic spots. Maps are available at certain accessible locations and at the forest headquarters about a quarter mile from the forest entrance.

In the Area

Fox Hunt Farms Gourmet Shop (South Woodstock): 203-928-0714

The Inn at Woodstock Hill (Woodstock): 203-928-0528

Mashamoquet Brook State Park (Pomfret): 203-566-2304 (Bureau of Parks and Forests, Hartford)

Pachaug State Forest headquarters (Voluntown): 203-376-4075

Pomfret School (Pomfret): 203-928-7969

Prudence Crandall House Museum (Canterbury): 203-546-9916; 203-566-3005

Roseland Cottage (Woodstock): 203-928-4074

Sandra Lee's Herbs and Everlastings (Pomfret): 203-974-0525

Vanilla Bean Cafe (Pomfret): 203-928-1562

Woodstock Orchards (Woodstock): 203-928-2225

2 ~

New Milford to Canaan, Connecticut

From Danbury and I-84 in the southeast section of the state: Take US 7 north to New Milford. This trip runs approximately forty-nine miles.

Highlights: Housatonic River valley, covered bridges at Bulls Bridge and West Cornwall, Kent Falls, Housatonic Meadows State Park, Great Falls in Falls Village, small towns, and many river views.

New Milford to Bulls Bridge

Not only does this trip take you through the river-edge country of the peacefully flowing Housatonic River, but it also follows the same easy highway all the way from New Milford to Canaan—US 7. One reason the route offers a relaxed rendezvous with rural life is that no hint of a city—not even of a large small town—can be seen nearby on a map. This northwest corner of the state speaks to the rustic counterpart of the masterly industrial side of Connecticut, located especially along the congested southern ocean strip and central core of Hartford.

14

Because of this isolation, Danbury becomes the only big-city access point to the New Milford starting point. But Danbury is also a good reminder of the long manufacturing history of the state. Known as "Hat City," Danbury during the 1930s produced millions of felt hats from its fifty-one hat factories for millions of men across the nation. The era of the dress hat, of course, has disappeared, and with it have gone the hat factories. But Danbury holds another surprise in its history: the birthplace and home of Charles Ives (1874–1954), whom some musical historians and critics consider the preeminent American composer of the twentieth century. Ives was a different kind of ingenious "Connecticut Yankee," not of the ilk of Seth Thomas, who made clocks; Samuel Colt, who produced the revolvers that won the Wild West; Charles Goodyear, whose vulcanized rubber tires transported America; and Eli Whitney, whose cotton gin dressed the nation. Ives's genius produced innovative vanguard music before Arnold Schoenberg and Igor Stravinsky had their say. He was a spirit unto himself in the great New England American creative tradition, a man who literally heard a different drummer, and all the other instrumentalists besides. His compositions *Unanswered Question, Sunday in Central Park,* and the *Concord Sonata* are performed often now, although during his life they were scarcely played at all. His masterpiece, the Fourth Symphony, exhibits such a range of musical invention and individuality that the symphony is sometimes described as among the supreme American compositions of all time. In fact, Ives's Fourth Symphony is called the best musical description of America ever produced and includes scenes of formality and refinement along with raucous democracy and social chaos.

When you drive the ten miles north on US 7 to New Milford this knowledge of Danbury puts the city you're leaving and the area you're entering into perspective. Begin this excursion by veering to the left on US 7 as US 202 turns right over the Housatonic River to New Milford on the other side of the bridge. After passing through a section of scattered buildings, you'll soon sense that you're heading into the countryside. A mile up the road the power company on the right reminds you that the Housatonic, modestly sized as it is, continues to play a role here and at other locations upriver in providing electrical power to the area.

In another mile and a half State 37 appears abruptly on the left, but you continue on US 7 north. For the next three miles or so, drive along the banks of the Housatonic. The road winds through the thick woods and, being narrow with sometimes scarcely a shoulder, slows the speed and the spirit. Unfortunately, the river hides behind a long thick scrim of trees (except in leafless winter). Once in a while glimpses of water-sparkles flash through the brush and tree trunks, but on the whole your enjoyment of the river consists more in knowing it flows close by than in seeing it.

As you approach Gaylordsville, a turnout overlooking the river on the right comes up fast, but don't worry about missing it. Up ahead you'll get to the river edge soon enough. In the meantime, US 7 leads you over a bridge and suddenly you're into Gaylordsville, a pleasant bend-in-the-river town. Be sure to look for the giant sycamore trees with their sleek, speckled trunks and rich green foliage. Several of these wonderful trees stand imperially erect by the edge of the main street, which you're on.

As you move farther into town, which isn't moving *that* far in this village, you can't miss Aaron's Antiques on the right and the 1854 Methodist Church on a knoll to the left. Then immediately before you cross the new concrete bridge over the river, slow down and turn onto the downward asphalt ramp to the side of the Housatonic. This open spot gives you a good chance to get out and stretch a few minutes, maybe eat a snack, explore the grassy parklike banks of the river, or sit and study with all your might the mesmerizing waters as the pretty Housatonic tumbles politely over the boulders.

You could spend some time walking the town, too. On the other side of the bridge the Gaylordsville Market and the U.S. Post Office, across from the volunteer fire department in a semicircular setting, is a well-stocked small-town store, an inviting place to pick up food and supplies for the miles ahead.

From the bridge, with the Housatonic River on the left now, US 7 takes you through the trees on a rather winding road with virtually no shoulder for about the next two miles to the Kent town line. About a half mile later the four corners of Bulls Bridge appear. Here lies another dam complex of Northeast Utilities, and you'll notice as you approach the four corners a series of constructed banks and reservoirs.

Be sure to turn left at the corners; the covered bridge is visible. It's a short, plain, older bridge that crosses the smallish but dramatic complex of waterpower with its bare-rock chutes and gouged-out canyons. Also, immediately on the other side of the bridge a parking area allows you to get out of your car again and maybe take a short hike along a well-routed trail in the Bulls Bridge Development. The area is designed for hiking, fishing, picnicking, and canoeing; maps are available.

After enjoying this compact scenic overlook, drive a half mile or so farther west up this road. You'll pass some backwater feeds to the Housatonic River system and maybe spot some ducks in the tight wetlands. If you keep straight on the road, the "Farm at Bulls Bridge" comes up on the right—a well-kept, attractive spread in the back hills. This road, in fact, takes you into New York; that's how far west you are. But return to the covered bridge and the four corners of Bulls Bridge at US 7 north.

Kent to West Cornwall Covered Bridge

For 1.8 miles north on US 7 from Bulls Bridge, you follow long stretches of open views of the Housatonic River, an easygoing ride on a two-lane road that gets you into the spirit of the woods-and-river scene. When the road veers from the river, up ahead a short distance, open farmland takes its place, and then the Housatonic reappears. The alternating rhythm of river and farmland plays with you in this countryside, and that's part of the pleasure.

In a little more than another mile, you enter Kent, born in 1731 and still looking trim and active. The main street (US 7) runs between two sides of specialty shops that are sure to whet your appetite for a walking visit. The human-scale heart of the town invites leisurely strolls by and in the shops, up and down the well-heeled town, past the flowers and stately maples.

Near the corner where the Saint Andrew's 1826 Episcopal Church stands, you'll find the House of Books, the Kent Coffee & Chocolate Company, Golden Thistle Antiques, the Stroble Bakery, clothing stores, restaurants, and real estate offices. The bakery, for instance, exudes the sweet-smelling aromas of "Old Fashioned Goodness Baked in Our Kitchen Every Day," the kind of small-scale, big-flavor shop where you see the bakers rolling and shaping breads, coffee cakes, and sweet rolls galore. Then scarcely a step away you can watch chocolatemaking in another open kitchen: fudges, candy truffles, chocolates of all sizes and shapes, not to mention the coffees and teas available for the road or to drink on the spot.

Less than a half mile north on US 7, the four-room, colonial Chaucer House, a bed and breakfast on the right, typifies some of the flavor of Kent not only by its sublime appearance but its very name indeed. Across the street don't miss the turreted, elaborate (for New England) First Congregational Church, "gathered in 1741," built in 1849.

A few minutes more north a treat awaits if you have the slightest interest in fascinating old tools the early settlers made and used to improve their lives. The Sloane-Stanley Museum, located on the same grounds as the old Kent Iron Furnace of the last century, displays all sorts of intriguing contraptions, some of them dating to the 1600s. Also on display are works by Eric Sloane, known widely for his series of hand-illustrated books describing the ingenious tools of yesteryear.

A couple of minutes more north outside town, US 7 bends to the left where Cobble Road enters at a stop sign. Turn here for a wonderful farm scene of red barns, a silo, and outbuildings, a working farm of fields sloping up and away. It's only two-tenths of a mile to Cobble Brook Farm. From 1739 this site grew into an early settlement centered around water, the magnet that empowered most of the early villages and towns. Rivers like the Housatonic provided transportation, food, a means of transferring timber, and water for irrigation of farms and gardens. In the case of small Cobble Brook, which still runs through here, water provided power for forges, a tannery, cider mills and gristmills, fulling mills, and sawmills. Here too congregated two churches, a school, general store, trading post, butcher and blacksmith shops, brickyard, animal pound, and burial and parade grounds, all because of the slant of the land that tumbles Cobble Brook water down the hills. But all is gone now except the brook and a historical marker of these energetic yesteryears.

Back on US 7 you pass some updated eighteenth-century homes, and then drive into shaded country and rolling hills. In 3.3 miles from the Cobble Road stop sign and immediately after descending a knoll, Kent Falls State Park appears on the right. You can't miss it, a perfect spot for a stroll through a charming pedestrian covered bridge that crosses Kent Falls Brook next to the parking lot. The 200-foot cascading falls are plainly visible to the rear, but take a few minutes to see them up close, especially in full-brim spring and early summer. Picnic tables are scattered widely around the expanses of mowed grass; rest rooms are available.

Once again on US 7 the road rises from the shallow falls valley and then leads you through more cruise-along country. In less than a mile the Cornwall township line appears (established in 1740), but in the area are Cornwall Bridge, West Cornwall, Cornwall Hollow, Cornwall Center, and just plain Cornwall. You're heading for the covered bridge at West Cornwall, not Cornwall Bridge village. Confusing it is. Just stay on US 7.

A couple of miles after the Cornwall township line, continue past State 45 on the right. A little over another mile, US 7 veers to the left and overlaps State 4 west a short distance across the Housatonic River. Veer right as you follow US 7 and enter Housatonic Meadows State Park.

The river flows on your right now, and in several locations along the next few miles (the first spot is right away at the entrance) you can get close to the Housatonic through boat-launching access and picnic areas. One of the choice scenes along this friendly river peeking through the trees now and then, and in just about any season, are people geared up in rubber waders and standing in the smooth-flowing water as they fly-cast for trout. The delicate S sweeps of their lines back and forth over the shallow river can mesmerize you with the silent artistry of an experienced wrist.

When you drive through this backcountry, the reason it's preserved becomes obvious. The road cuts through close-knit woods, turning in soft curves, and generally follows close by the river route itself.

In about 4.5 miles, State 128 enters on the right. Take the very short connector downhill to the wooden covered bridge you can't miss. Big, red, and sturdy, the bridge is a credit to Ithiel Town, who designed it in 1837. Foot traffic, horses and buggies, and now horseless carriages have been using the bridge ever since.

This 1837 covered bridge spans
the Housatonic River in West Cornwall

Cross to the east side of the Housatonic for a visit to the hillside village center. Cafés, sit-down inn restaurants, cabinetmakers' studios, pottery shops—this compact scene invites a stroll through the shops in well-aged buildings. Along the northeast side of the Housatonic here, some good open stretches make the bridge irresistible to camera buffs.

Falls Village and Canaan

Once you have gone back through the bridge and onto the east side of the Housatonic River, follow US 7 north into a few sections of the Housatonic State Forest. About 3.5 miles from the bridge, you cross the Salisbury township line. A mile later State 112 enters on the left, but veer right to stay on US 7. At this junction a small sign by the side of the highway indicates that the famed Appalachian Trail crosses here.

The Appalachian Trail follows the Housatonic River from Bulls Bridge, where it enters from New York, to Falls Village up ahead, where it turns toward Salisbury and heads north into Massachusetts. This trail is the premier hiking path in the country. Benton MacKaye, a man of vision who loved the outdoors, put forth the idea of the trail formally in an article in 1921 when he proposed that a footpath along the backbone of the Appalachian Mountain Range be cut through fourteen eastern states. These included Georgia, North Carolina, Tennessee, Virginia, West Virginia, Maryland, Pennsylvania, New Jersey, New York, Connecticut, Massachusetts, Vermont, New Hampshire, and Maine.

The extraordinary idea ignited immediate enthusiasm and action among members of individual hiking clubs along the proposed route. The following year the first stretch was prepared and marked in the Palisades Interstate Park in New York. Originally estimated to stretch 1,200 miles, the trail ended up more than 2,000 miles long when it was completed in 1937. Thanks to honorable volunteer work to maintain the trail, millions of Americans hike some section of the fabled footpath every year. Some people set goals of hiking different sections of the trail year after year until they complete the entire 2,000 miles. Fewer still hike the entire trail end-to-end at one time. These thru-hikers, as they're called, follow the white blazes on tree trunks and rocks all the way from Springer Mountain in Georgia to Mount Katahdin in central Maine, usually in about four to five months.

The trail leads hikers into the gulches of the South, the notches of the North, across shallow rivers and into rocky gorges, inside rhododendron thickets and along open ridgelines. Thru-hikers walk through all kinds of weather from snow flurries to 100-plus-degree weather, not to mention thunderstorms, flooded rivers, and dried-up springs. The adventure of the Appalachian Trail, no matter in what size doses it is hiked, imprints anyone's memory of wilderness walking with enough satisfaction and joy to enkindle the appetite for more.

Benton MacKaye wrote about the significance of his Appalachian Trail: "The old pioneer opened through a forest a path for the spread of civilization. His work was nobly done and life of the town and city is in consequence well upon the map throughout our country. Now comes the great task of holding this life in check—for it is just as bad to have too much urbanization as too little. America needs her forest and her wild places quite as much as her cities and her settled places."

In 1969 Congress designated the Appalachian Trail a National Scenic Trail. After years of rerouting and purchases of private land parcels, the trail now covers more than 161,000 acres (in a long line), and most of the early road-walking has been eliminated. Through the National Trails System Act, the Appalachian Trail comes under the jurisdiction of the secretary of the interior, with the U.S. Forest Service assuming responsibility for those parts of the trail that pass over Forest

Service land. Individual hiking clubs continue to maintain sections of the trail within their states. These clubs join to form the Appalachian Trail Conference, which organizes and coordinates trail-related matters.

All this lies behind the meaning of that small sign "Appalachian Trail" by the side of the road. It's a reminder of how one man's vision and the concerted action of others can create a lasting gift to millions of people.

In about another mile veer to the left for a short bypass into Falls Village, a largely white-building center overlooking the Housatonic River. This was part of the larger-area town of Canaan, established in 1738; this settlement became known as Falls Village because of the nearby Great Falls of the river. But 120 years later the town was divided into Canaan and North Canaan. To make matters thoroughly confusing to travelers, the town of Canaan (up the road) is located in the North Canaan township.

Nevertheless, Falls Village has always been a resource town, featuring lumber mills and gristmills in 1741, ironworks in 1743, a fulling mill in 1747. Falls Village supplied iron ore, limestone, and lumber for the Revolutionary and Civil Wars, and a power-company dam was built there in 1912 to take advantage of the cascades that thrust the Housatonic waters into high speed.

The Great Falls lie one mile from the T junction of the main street of the town center. Turn right at the T junction, then two-tenths of a mile later turn left at Water Street and drive under the bridge. Veer to the right downhill to the power-station complex in sight now and go past the station, turning left over the bridge. Follow the main road a half mile (don't be tempted by any side roads posted with "No Outlet" signs). The scenic overlooks are on the right; they give good views of the white water tumbling past.

Return the same way to Falls Village center. Then steer up Main Street past the Canaan town offices on the right. Stay on this road as it curves uphill slightly past the David M. Hunt Library, a large red-brick building on the right. A short distance farther and you come to US 7. Turn left, and drive the remaining 5.5 pleasant and easy miles to end the trip at Canaan.

In the Area

Bulls Bridge Development, Northeast Utilities (Hartford): 203-665-5315

Chaucer House Bed and Breakfast (Kent): 203-927-4858

David M. Hunt Library (Falls Village): 203-824-7424

Gaylordsville Market (Gaylordsville): 203-355-3740

Golden Thistle Antiques (Kent): 203-354-5801

House of Books (Kent): 203-927-4104

Kent Coffee & Chocolate Company (Kent): 203-927-1445

Sloane-Stanley Museum and Kent Furnace (Kent): 203-927-3849; 203-566-3005

Stroble Bakery (Kent): 203-927-4073.

3 ~

Salisbury to Granby

From Great Barrington, Massachusetts: Take State 41 south through South Egremont, Massachusetts, to Salisbury, Connecticut. From Torrington, Connecticut, take State 4 to Sharon, then State 41 north to Salisbury. This trip runs approximately forty-nine miles.

Highlights: Attractive small towns, working dairy farms, Yale University summer music festival in Norfolk, Hitchcock chair factory, 1796 Riverton Inn, state forests, Barkhamstead Reservoir.

Salisbury to Canaan

Main Street in the center of Salisbury invites a take-your-time walk through this genteel town of about 4,000 residents, a good way to begin this trip. At the south end of the town center you can't miss the imposing granite-block Scoville Memorial Library situated on a grass-and-tree corner. North across the street stands the inevitably white Congregational Church, gathered in 1744, built in 1800. Straight west across the street is the new town hall, and then back diagonally on the east side of the street the chamber of commerce uses a stalwart red-brick building that was originally Salisbury Academy, built in 1833. There you have it—in less than a block: the core of New England village life of the mind, the soul, the town government, the learning youth of the future.

Farther on, the merchants in small, independent shops line the easy boulevard: clothiers, grocers, pharmacists, innkeepers, booksellers. Next to the Salisbury Pharmacy a passageway bearing the sign "The Marketplace of Salisbury" leads you to several other small businesses, including the Epicure Market, in the rear of which you'll find a tempting bakery and delicatessen. Connected to the back of the pharmacy you'll find a charming little shop offering ice creams and coffees.

Be sure to stop here too at Lion's Head Books. Owned and operated by Mike McCabe, who has been a bookseller in Salisbury for twenty years, the shop carries an appealing mix of current titles, secondhand books, and some specialty first editions. McCabe operates Lion's Head Books in a small redesigned house where his wares are displayed in cozy nooks and rooms. Besides catering to travelers on four wheels, he also befriends the two-footed hikers of the Appalachian Trail, which crosses through Salisbury's outskirts. End-to-end trail hikers have special book needs. One booted pair came into his shop some years ago and, after much browsing and discussion of whether to add weight on their shoulders, ended up buying a book with the fewest ounces and the heaviest punch—Robinson Jeffers's selected poems in a small paperback.

Like many towns in the area, Salisbury was born before the Revolution, and, again similar to others in the region, developed its iron-ore resources into a major production along with agriculture. The first blast furnace in the state was built two decades later in Lakeville, two miles south. This iron-producing industry played its important role in the Revolutionary War, the War of 1812, and the development of the iron horse and the network of iron rails spreading across the continent in the nineteenth century, as well as the iron-related industries that followed the railroads. Iron production here, in fact, lasted until the 1900s.

When you're ready to get back on the road, head north on Main Street the short distance to the Y junction at the end of the town center. The White Hart Inn, an appealing old-timer with white-cloth service, faces you from the middle of the Y. State 41 is on the left, US 44 on the right. You can take 44 east to Canaan, but if you wish a short detour steer up State 41 four or five miles for some lovely rolling countryside with pleasant homes, farms, and woods. You'll see peaceful Connecticut views, lolling horses, cleared fields interspersed with blocks of mixed hardwood and pines.

Otherwise, head straight up US 44 east at the Y junction. In a short time the terrain slants upward a little until two miles later Salisbury School appears in its nostalgic red-brick hilltop scene. This easygoing ride moves you through more farm fields, alongside swamp ponds, and past well-seasoned houses, some perked up for today, others left to fade gray with the ineluctable years.

About four miles from Salisbury junction, US 44 crosses the Housatonic River, the dominant body of the ubiquitous flowing water in the northwestern section of the state. The Housatonic translates into three major uses—electrical power, fly-fishing, and scenic views, not necessarily in that order. As you cross the low-sided bridge, the river meanders by, its tree-hugging shore green and lush in summer, brown and open with its leafless, bony tree trunks in winter. In either season the river looks lazy here, almost belittling its own long-range worth and might.

On the other side of the bridge State 126 south comes in on the right; stay on US 44, veering to the left as it takes you by clusters of houses. For about another mile the Housatonic parallels the road. Another mile and the Canaan townline sign appears, and then more houses, obvious clues that you're approaching town. A half mile more, turn right on US 44 and then steer straight as US 7 overlaps US 44 into the heart of Canaan, a busy, compact crossroads town a short distance from Massachusetts to the north.

Immediately after going straight past the core corners of Canaan where US 7 turns north, turn right into Canaan Union

*The Housatonic Railroad still chugs past
the depot at Canaan Union Station*

Station. You can't miss it. The yellow L-shaped station sits by the side of the tracks with a bright red caboose parked permanently at one end. The 1872 depot is touted as the oldest station in continuous use in the nation. Nowadays it's partitioned into local businesses—a printing shop, accounting offices, a craft store. The Housatonic Railroad still chugs through town on scenic cruises, eventually and slowly clicking the tracks beside the Housatonic River after the train reaches Falls Village. You can hop aboard during summer, but if you're planning to do so always telephone ahead. Sometimes major blocks of the schedule are eliminated and rides may be available only in the fall foliage season.

In the meantime, you have two picturesque places to eat at the station: the Pub 'N' Grub and Collin's Diner. The Pub 'N' Grub, located on the left end of the station, serves lunch and dinner and sports a wonderfully long, eye-dazzling shiny wood bar in the old grand saloon style. Tables are set in an adjoining porch. Part of the fun of eating here is the combination of a sensible menu and the pub atmosphere.

Collin's Diner, serving since 1941, catches the eye, too, with its blue-and-silver train carlike shape, so appropriate for the depot. The diner, with Mike Hamzy as proprietor, stands by itself at the left of the parking lot entrance, and if any diner deserves an admiring look and a visit, this is it—Collin's is a classic sight. Inside, the place is cozy and clean, and the food is tasty.

As you head back onto US 44 east out of town, remember that Canaan, first settled by Dutch and English, was also part of the network of iron-ore blast furnaces in this corner of Connecticut. For two centuries Canaan produced pig iron and everything from nails to ship anchors. Like Salisbury, Canaan had its outlying subsettlements tied into the grid of iron producers in one form or another. Those days are gone, but the memories of this iron legacy linger long in this pocket of the state.

In less than a half mile from Union Station, US 7 turns south at the signal light; remain on US 44 east as it continues straight ahead. But if you're hungry for a bakery treat, immediately turn right into Christiansen's Bakery and Cafe, a modest-looking coffee shop with a "baked here" bakery. You'll discover not megafactory-style "eats" but a flaky apple turnover with real kitchen taste.

Norfolk to Riverton

For the next seven miles or so to Norfolk, follow the Blackberry River up as the waters flow down. Much of this back-country harbors shallow, secretive valleys and enclaves, some of them with dairy farms, others with loosely knit housing settlements. You pass places with picture-book names: Blackberry River Inn (from the late 1700s), Elm Knoll Farm, Laurelbrook Farm. Two and a half miles along the road, US 44 suddenly crests a small rise in the terrain and there across a long sweep of a field stands the North Canaan Congregational Church, a striking New England scene. The simplicity of the façade, the leanness of the tall steeple with a sparkling gold ball on the weather vane, the separateness of the church surrounded by grass and a narrow byway curving away from the front and side of the white building make for an eye-catcher of the first degree.

Another mile up the road and into the hills, a large turnout allows you to park, get out, stretch, and take a closer look at the Blackberry River tumbling relentlessly over the boulders.

Then another half mile farther on and up, the outskirts of Norfolk appear and after another half mile, US 44 veers right past the Immaculate Conception Catholic Church. This is the kind of building that will draw inevitable comments one way or the other. The bottom half of fieldstone supports the top half of pink scalloplike stucco. You cannot miss it.

A short distance to the top of the hill brings you to the Norfolk center green, which is surrounded by handsome principal buildings of church, state, and university. You'll want to park and walk around here, an attractive, cultivated town center with the 145-year-old National Iron Bank (ever see a name like that?) a block away. At the southern end of the green the entrance to the Yale University Summer School of Art and Music leads to the music shed where many great and renowned performers have appeared.

Be sure to take an inside look at the red-brick public library on the north end of the green. Its wood vaulted ceiling and mezzanine with spindle railing will lift your eyes and spirits both.

A walk around the left (east) side of the green takes you past the Norfolk Historical Museum, open to the public. The simple 1840 white building was originally designed as Norfolk Academy and then later turned into the town hall and jail.

Set in the Berkshire Hills, Norfolk in its isolation developed a curious history as the outside world came through and eventually remained here. Settled in 1744, forty-four voting residents declared the community incorporated fourteen years later. Over the next few decades news of the deteriorating conditions between the English Crown and the New World colonists reached Norfolk by travelers on the Hartford-Albany turnpike; Norfolk was a tavern and inn stop along the route. When the shot heard 'round the world was fired in April 1775, twenty-four Norfolk men took up arms and marched to Boston in support of the colonial uprising. The number increased to 150 Norfolk men fighting in the Revolutionary War.

After the Revolution, life settled back again into hardscrabble farming in the rolling, boulder-strewn bottomland and highland clearings. More and more lumber mills and gristmills were constructed, many of them using waterpower from the Blackberry River, which dominates the area. In the

32

1800s industry grew and from the region came linseed oil, woolens, men's hats, cheeseboxes, scythes. Then when the numbers of farmers and manufacturers declined and they departed for other times and places, Norfolk turned into a well-known summer colony. During the last of the 1800s the public library was built, Yale University came to town, and the Litchfield County Choral Union was formed. Today the town is replete with many fine old country homes turned into bed and breakfasts, a few of them two-century-old colonials, others Victorian and Tudor.

The next fifteen miles to Riverton take you through pleasant country roads of easy driving, although you do have to steer through Winsted, a nice enough city but congested. Before Winsted, the roads cover much likeable country, including the first six or seven miles west of Norfolk. US 44 leads you on a stretch of highland roadway through mixed woodlands, with a few small farmsteads en route but mostly maples, oaks, spruce, and pines. Colebrook and Winchester town lines come and go. No hurrying required.

When you curve downhill toward Winsted, remain on US 44 all the way into the center of the city. Signs for State 183 and State 263 appear on the outskirts of Winsted; keep on US 44. It's not confusing, just a bit more citified as you approach the main thoroughfare through the increasing signs of traffic, taller buildings, and signal lights.

You curve more downward into the main business district of Winsted. As you do, look for State 8 north toward the farther end of the main shopping area. The signs are clear, and State 8 comes at a signal light.

Turn left onto State 8 north, which takes you right away past a long green—a rather long, narrow park. A little more than 2.5 miles on State 8, turn right onto State 20 east—back into the woodlands and home free.

After 2.25 miles of some moderately winding backcountry-road driving, suddenly the Riverton line appears and you cross a low bridge over the West Branch of the Farmington River. Another half mile and you curve into Riverton, home of the original factory of the legendary Hitchcock chair. The John Tarrent Kenney Hitchcock Museum of rare nineteenth-century Hitchcock furniture, housed in a reconverted church, is readily seen as part of this small-town complex. Up ahead a very short distance is the showroom of the Hitchcock manufacturing plant that displays some of its old working techniques, including hand methods still used today.

Beside the Farmington River in 1818 Lambert Hitchcock first operated his chair factory to overnight success. The chairmaker became so renowned that later he was elected state senator and became known as coming from Hitchcockville. The famous Hitchcock chair originally was a strong and simple design, sturdy and stenciled with gold paint, some chairs with cane, others with solid wood seats. The rush seats were made of cattails from the banks of the Farmington River. Boston and Cape Cod rockers, as they were known, also grew in such widespread popularity that the name Hitchcock for many grew equivalent to the concept of a chair.

The museum is located in the Old Union Church, which Hitchcock himself helped build in 1829. He and others in town used hand-cut granite and nearby chestnut and oak timber. You'll find many examples of antique painted furniture by other woodworkers besides Hitchcock from the 1700s and 1800s. A fifteen-minute video titled *America Be Seated* tells the Hitchcock tale. Seeing the demonstrations at the Hitchcock factory showrooms a short walk away makes an intriguing and instructive stop. You'll enjoy the explanation of weaving, rushing, woodworking, and stenciling.

As you drive over the river again to the stop sign, the 1796 Old Riverton Inn, a colonial stagecoach stop, faces you.

34

A charming place, the inn in the early days was owned first by Jesse Ives and, therefore, was known on the Hartford-Albany post route as the Ives Tavern and the Ives Hotel. Dining is open to the public for lunch and dinner. The low-ceilinged, wood-beamed, all-white Colonial Dining Room takes your imagination back to the tavern days when such a place was heaven-sent after bone-bumping traveling on interminably bouncing stagecoach rides.

Hartland to Granby

Following State 20 to Hartland finds you right away alongside more of the Farmington River with the Hitchcock furniture factory on the opposite bank. Then into the woods you go and climb with the tree-crowded hills. The road is narrow and sometimes winding for the next 3.5 miles or so to the stop sign at the junction with State 181, where you turn left.

In another half mile you enter Hartland, a remote-feeling, pleasantly spaced small town that stretches with an openness along State 20. Somehow this nicely staged town slows you down to enjoy the leisurely looking scene. A little farther on, some attractive farmhouses catch your eye, but don't miss the long view on the right here where the woods have been cleared and the far reaches of northern Connecticut roll on, one soft hill ridge after another.

This is secluded country you're entering—Peoples State Forest back at Riverton, Tunxis State Forest here around Hartland. Wilderness schools and camps are secreted off the highways. Rough roads and trails meander into the mountainous land. The area is out of the way, off the asphalt track mostly. It's its own reward. So two miles from that long eastward view in Hartland, suddenly after a mile-long drive through a tunnel of trees a narrow swath of blue water appears far below in

35

a steep-sided canyon. This is Barkhamsted Reservoir. The reservoir is irresistible, and enough room is available to pull over, park, and get out for an admiring look at the V cleft of the terrain that cuts the earth below.

As you descend the mountainside somewhat steeply but on an easily driveable road, small waterfalls on the left cascade, especially in spring and early summer. On the right some flashing blue views of the reservoir squeeze through the trees. In a couple miles you come to the northern tip of the reservoir and the bottom flat of the land. State 20 hooks you around the tip of the lake, and then faster than you anticipate up you climb again. The climb angles at a sensible rise, easy to drive and mostly straight away.

By the time you breach the top of the terrain, less than a mile of flat roadway takes you into East Hartland to a stop sign. Turn left and then right almost immediately; simply follow the State 20 signs, and continue to do so past State 219.

From the State 219 turnoff, State 20 leads you through more backcountry calm for the next seven miles or so to Granby. The houses appear more and more as you approach the end of the trip, but in the meantime you'll definitely enjoy the softly downhill drive as you parallel the boulder-splashing West Branch Salmon Brook through the thick and thin of rural life.

In the Area

Chamber of Commerce (Salisbury): 203-435-0740

Christiansen's Bakery and Cafe (Canaan): 203-824-5544

Collin's Diner (Canaan): 203-824-7040

Epicure Market (Salisbury): 203-435-2559

Hitchcock Museum (Riverton): 203-738-4950

Housatonic Railroad (Canaan): 203-824-0339
Lion's Head Books (Salisbury): 203-435-9328
Old Riverton Inn (Riverton): 203-379-8678
Pub 'N' Grub (Canaan): 203-824-4848
Scoville Memorial Library (Salisbury): 203-435-2838
White Hart Inn (Salisbury): 203-435-0030

4 ~

New Milford to Burlington

From Danbury: Take US 7 north to New Milford.

Highlights: Housatonic River, New Milford green, New Preston village, Lake Waramaug, Mount Tom State Park, White Memorial Conservation Center, historic Litchfield, small towns, woodlands. This trip runs approximately forty-three miles.

New Milford to New Preston

Called the Litchfield Hills, the northwest corner of Connecticut is named after an alluring town on this trip—Litchfield. But before reaching this grandly historic stop, other sights along the way definitely shouldn't be missed.

As you turn right from US 7 onto the steel bridge from a rather mallish junction with US 202, something wonderfully unexpected awaits you right away. As soon as you cross over the bridge toward the center of New Milford (population 24,000), turn left onto Youngs Field Road. Suddenly, a long,

38

lofty row of willows appears beside the edge of the Housatonic River you crossed. With a large town playing field on the right-hand side of the road, this short, congenial scene clips off the bluster of business traffic you encountered a minute ago. The appealing invitation here is that the Housatonic ("Place Beyond the Mountains") flows its hefty width almost at road level. The river curves into sight from around a wooded bend up ahead and slides close to the single-line stand of willows. A picnic table sits a few tempting feet from the water. This river-edge strip makes a pleasant stroll cut off from the asphalt world. Water and land meet with no bank in between, making it easy for you to enjoy the scene up close. Only a minute into this trip you've seen a harbinger of more to come in these foothills of the Berkshire Mountains.

Once back on US 202 toward the town of New Milford, settled in 1707, turn left at the first street, which is plainly identified by the old "New Milford Railroad Depot." The station now houses the chamber of commerce and the Commission on the Arts. This street, where the railroad chugged into town for generations, still exudes the riverfront feeling of New Milford, which, at sixty-five square miles, is the largest town in land size in Connecticut. A few old-time lamppost replicas are stationed along the way, but overall this street is lined with mostly old brick buildings—small businesses, restaurants and cafés, a smoke-and-read shop.

Continue down this street a short distance and turn right up Boardman Terrace. A block uphill takes you to the midpoint of the engaging town green, long, useful, and sprouting a variety of grandfatherly deciduous trees. The far side of the green is lined with large, white, stately wooden houses (now businesses) and stone churches. One of the benefits of the New England sense of history is the frequent refurbishing or remodeling of the grand old homes of yesteryear into businesses of today, far better than demolishing fine irreplaceable examples of Greek Revival or Federal-style architecture in the name of urban renewal. You won't see any bulldozing along this green. Instead, this town center combines the refreshed aesthetics of past centuries with the hurry-along pace of our era.

You have to turn right on this one-way side of the green, which takes you to Bridge Street (the main street that you first used). Turn left and go downhill for about a tenth of a mile to the stop sign, where you take another left, continuing onto US 202. For the next mile or so the road climbs out of town. At the top of the easy hill the valley view to your right gives you the dual sense of being in the country while still close to town. A little more than another mile and you're definitely out of town.

For the next four miles the driving is pleasant, with scattered small businesses close to the road and some picturesque sights surprising you now and then. Several houses come fast into view on the right that are built tiptoe alongside a narrow, rushing brook channeled through granite chutes and under narrow bridges. Willows and maples droop their branches over the water. Once past the Northville town line you'll pass four small horse farms, barns and stables, and probably see the grays and roans lolling in the fields.

One-tenth of a mile past the Washington town line you can't miss the Reid & Wright Antiquarian Book Center on the right. An elaborate, glossy, wooden entrance calls your attention right away to this barnlike book building, an appealing stop for sure. Inside you step down onto an oriental rug, a glass chandelier overhead, a long "greeting" table directly in front. Stalls of books line the walls and center of the building, an inviting place.

This stop features another surprise—Coffee Espress. In the same parking lot, a kiosk offers a tantalizing array of coffee direct to your car. This drive-through coffee shop opened recently as one of the first in the East, although these coffee stops are popular in the Pacific Northwest. Besides straight espresso and café au lait, the kiosk brews a long line of coffee styles and flavors. Regular coffee and tea are on the menu as well. You can order anything from cappuccino and con panna (espresso topped with whipped cream) to Moo (steamed milk topped with foam) and No Fun (an espresso made with low-fat milk and decaf espresso).

Back on US 202 and after crossing the Marbledale town line in about a tenth of a mile, with scattered businesses and homes along the way, less than a half mile later an intriguing red house, now an antique store, appears on the left. The large extended roof shows that once it was, as the sign says, a "Coach Stop."

A mile later State 45 on the left angles in at forty-five degrees. Be sure to take this to New Preston. Follow State 45 uphill and you'll come to a delightful, updated small-town center. Ten years ago this sleepy town didn't wake up until high noon, and its offering included little more than a general store, a church steeple, and an old mill. Then a few venturesome new businesses opened up, and others followed until now, and the town is alive and up early in the morning again. Many antique stores (J. Seitz & Co. is one interesting example) and restaurants and cafés now spark up New Preston.

From the bottom of the hill on US 202 you may have seen through the trees on your left an unusually tall church steeple high on the hillside. Now that you're in New Preston, take a closer look. Continue up the short main street and turn left on New Preston Hill Road immediately before the yellow Pavilion Hall building, which faces you and the rest of the main street. Drive uphill to Church Street next on your left; follow this to the church, which now is in plain view.

The New Preston Congregational Church was established in 1757, and the building was erected in 1853. Up close the narrow, very tall steeple in a simple nineteenth-century rural style represents one obvious era. The low-crouching, modern building of the Washington Montessori School directly across the road represents another. It's a curious juxtaposition worth remembering in the current context in which New Preston finds itself.

Continue around on Church Street, which leads you back down to the center of town. Again you'll cross over a narrow, deep chute of water used by the old mill upriver. To get to this remnant of a bygone time, turn left up the main street again, but this time veer to the right and continue up State 45 past Pavilion Hall. In two-tenths of a mile on the left below at river edge, the old red mill stands dormant in the crowded trees. Plans are to revive the building and open it to the public.

A little farther up the hill, Lake Waramaug suddenly appears. Cruising along the lake edge makes a nice drive.

To return to US 202, retrace your route through New Preston and downhill a short way to the stop sign. Turn left onto US 202 and continue into country that opens up a little more.

Mount Tom State Park to White Memorial Conservation Center

From New Preston, the 4.5 miles to Mount Tom State Park (223 acres) are pleasant driving. Simply remain on US 202 as you pass turnoffs to State 47 and State 341.

The sign to the park directs you to the right onto an earthen road past Chenqueka, a large private summer camp with many outbuildings and playing fields. Mount Tom State Park is two-tenths of a mile down the road to the entrance kiosk. This modest park offers a swimming beach, a hot-food-and-cold-drink booth, and picnic tables lakeside as well as in the woods up the hill behind the parking lot. This might be a rest spot along your route, maybe a place to eat in the cool outdoors.

If you are not stopping, continue on US 202 past the Litchfield town line almost a mile later. Before long you enter Bantam and need to slow down as you proceed through this small outlying community.

About two miles after Bantam you'll definitely want to stop at the White Memorial Conservation Center, with signs on the right and an impressive half-mile entrance drive that silently counsels you into this private nature enclave.

At the parking lot an open-roofed display summarizes what these dedicated grounds are all about: "Recreation. Education. Conservation. Research."

By all means, visit the museum in the large, home-style building a short walk from the display and up the path. Many exhibits and dioramas illustrate the intricate workings of nature and wildlife. More than 30,000 people enjoy the museum every year.

This far-seeing enterprise began generations ago and is traced to the John Jay White family that summered in Litchfield in 1863. Their children, brother Alain and sister May, remembered enjoying this country so much that between 1908 and 1912, they bought 4,000 acres of it. A year later they established a nonprofit trust—The White Memorial Foundation—in memory of their parents, and this formed the basis of what gratifies and befriends visitors today. In 1964 the foundation was developed into the center, its core situated in the summer home of Alain and May White. The Whites also gave 6,000 other acres in parts of western Connecticut to the state, which in turn formed the nucleus of the state-parks-and-forests system.

Over the years the center has developed extensive programs; the public is welcome to participate. Facilities and programs available include tenting, campgrounds, and thirty-five miles of trails for hiking, cross-country skiing, and horse-back riding. Boardwalk trails allow bird-watching near a marsh pond. Picnicking, fishing, and boating on Bantam Lake and Bantam River are also encouraged. A section is set aside for orienteering, the sport and art of map and compass. All sorts and sizes of halls are available for meetings and conferences. An outdoor amphitheater can be used for campfire programs. Field trips, lectures, summer programs for children, and nature study courses are also part of the center program.

Although you may not wish to sign up or have the time to do so for these offerings, you can at least visit the first-rank museum and either walk or drive briefly through the welcoming grounds. The acres are mixed with fields and woods, ponds and brooks. As you drive out the grounds road past the museum/information center, the road takes you through some of these woods and by marshes to a connecting street; turn left to reach US 202 again.

Litchfield

Once you are back on US 202, continue east, passing on the left the stately white Litchfield Inn set back to the far end of a long green lawn. In another 1.5 miles steer uphill slightly to Litchfield green, celebrated for its broad, handsome length as the centerpiece of an important historic town.

Litchfield remains a lively, vital town of more than 8,000 with prideful links and recognition of its critical importance to the development of Connecticut and indeed the country. John Marsh of Hartford first explored this part of the state in 1715 when this frontier was known as "greenwoods" and "Western Lands" by the whites and "Bantam" by the Potauck nation. About five years later the town was settled and grew steadily in population and importance until 1751, when Litchfield was designated the county seat. As a crossroads location for stagecoach travel and freighting between New York and New England towns, Litchfield prospered.

During the Revolutionary War the village served as a supply depot for the Continental Army and a prison camp for captured loyalists. The town was situated to advantage as a supplier for American forces in the Hudson River Valley when the British were threatening Connecticut coast stations. And certainly without missing a beat, Litchfield history proclaims that in 1780 General George Washington slept here.

Many impressive "firsts" occurred in Litchfield. One of the most far-reaching and influential was the law school that Tapping Reeve established in 1784, the first law school in the new nation. Judge Reeve conducted lectures in law in his home parlor for two years, but when students outnumbered the square feet he built a one-room schoolhouse next to his home. He married Sally Burr, and taught law to his brother-in-law Aaron Burr, who eventually became vice president of the new United States. Reeve's law school spread its weight and persuasiveness from the little schoolhouse deep into the fabric of the emerging nation. The graduates included two vice presidents, six cabinet members, twenty-six U.S. senators, more than one hundred congressmen, sixteen governors, and three Supreme Court justices, not to mention the educator Horace Mann, painter George Catlin, and inventor Sydney E. Morse. Tours of the Tapping Reeve House and Law School are open to the public.

Another notable first includes the Sarah Pierce Litchfield Female Academy, established in 1792 as one of the pioneering schools for young women. Pierce's idea was "to ornament their minds" and to unite the academic and ornamental subjects of needlework, art, and music for women. She believed that men and women carried equal intellectual abilities and that both men and women would be happier if their potential were fully developed. In its forty-one-year history, the academy enrolled more than 3,000 students from the

American states and territories, Canada, and the West Indies. More than 50 percent of the students came from out of state. With the Tapping Reeve Law School full of mostly single young men in town, Sarah Pierce's academy of young women made a natural complement for Litchfield and provided a variety of "entertainments." More than sixty marriages resulted from students of the two schools.

By 1810 Litchfield ranked as the fourth largest town in the state, but because of its hilltop geography, the network of railroads bypassed the town. Its Golden Age from the Revolution to the 1830s was fast approaching an end, but the town was an exciting, vital intellectual center of Federalist New England. The legacies of its residents and students linger on—Ethan Allen, John C. Calhoun, Harriet Beecher Stowe, Oliver Walcott.

Many historic and aesthetic sights fill Litchfield for visitors to enjoy. The Reeve house and school, for example, are designated as a National Historic Landmark by the U.S. Department of the Interior, as are many other places. The town's historic district became the first one established in Connecticut by a special act of the General Assembly in 1959; the entire district includes more than 475 buildings and is also listed on the National Register of Historic Places.

The evolution of the famous three-century-old green reflects the persistent energy of the town. Created in 1723 as an early part of the town center, the green served as a wide crossroads for cattle drives and grazing. When Litchfield became the county seat, dignity arrived, too, and the green became the town park. During the Golden Age sycamore and elm trees were planted. By 1836 the green was divided into east and west parks, separated by crossroads. Over the years residents changed the pattern of lawns, planted more trees, and added fencing. During the Civil War recruitment for soldiers, presentation of colors, and parades for returning soldiers kept the green central to everyday Litchfield life. After

*First Congregational Church, built in 1721
on the town green of Litchfield*

the Civil War, the wooden fences disappeared and the surrounding architecture in many buildings changed from colonial to Gothic-style.

In the late 1870s corner streetlamps on the green were installed, more trees were planted, and iron-pipe fencing, concrete sidewalks, and tar paving appeared. The nearby fires of 1886 and 1888 razed many clapboard buildings; stores were rebuilt with brick. In 1907 Center Park became a small public garden with a Civil War cannon, a new flagpole, and a roadside watering trough and benches. Today the green remains a living part of Litchfield's extraordinary history.

You'll enjoy the buildings along both sides of the green: the 1721 First Congregational Church, the 1888 granite courthouse, the 1900 Litchfield Historical Society building with its rounded entrance. Founded in 1856, the historical society updated its facilities a few years ago. Both its permanent and moving exhibits offer an intriguing, sweeping panorama of a fascinating history. In a rear room of the museum, with striking copper doors, a clever mosaic in the center of the floor depicts the village around 1820 by houses and dates.

Harwinton to Burlington

Driving past the Litchfield Historical Society Museum on the right, the green on the left, continue straight ahead onto State 118 downhill. A half mile later on the left, you may wish to visit the Lourdes in Litchfield shrine, operated by the Montfort Missionaries. The thirty-five-acre shrine and grotto were built and opened in 1958 in honor of the vision of Mary, the Mother of Jesus, to Bernadette Soubirous in Lourdes, France, exactly one century earlier. The Montfort Missionaries are followers of Saint Louis de Montfort, a missionary priest of France in the early eighteenth century. The quarter-mile drive from the highway leads to a large parking lot. From there you can walk through a fieldstone arch to the grotto representing the place of the vision. Stations of the Cross depicting scenes of Jesus' suffering take you through a quarter mile of woods.

A large depiction of the Crucifixion is also visible near the grotto. A gift shop and picnic area are available.

Returning to State 118 east, continue easy, pleasant driving for the rest of the trip. Stay on State 118 for the next seven miles past State 8 and eventually straight onto State 4 east as you steer uphill to the center of Harwinton. Here you round a corner and suddenly see a nice country church and a down-home village center. On the other side of town another mile on the left, look for the large stone water trough inscribed on the top with "Erected 1906 by Newman Huncerford as a Memorial to his ancestor Abijah Catline lst. 1715–1778."

For the last two miles, remain on State 4 all the way. The Burlington town line comes up in two miles, and as you drive through this small town the backcountry feeling stays with you. About a mile on the far side of Burlington, a fish hatchery is open to the public down a short road on the right as part of the Nassahegon State Forest.

Otherwise, continue down a long, somewhat winding hillside through mixed woodlands to the large stop sign where State 4 runs into State 179.

In the Area

Coffee Espress (Marble Dale): 203-868-9971

J. Seitz & Co. (New Preston): 203-868-0119

Litchfield Historical Society (Litchfield): 203-567-4501

Litchfield Inn (Litchfield): 203-567-4503

Lourdes in Litchfield (Litchfield): 203-567-1041

New Milford Chamber of Commerce (New Milford):
    203-354-6080

New Milford Commission on the Arts (New Milford):
203-355-2873

Reid & Wright Antiquarian Book Center (New Preston):
203-868-7706

Tapping Reeve House and Law School (Litchfield):
203-567-4501

White Memorial Conservation Center (Litchfield):
203-567-0857

5 ~

Enfield to North Woodstock

From Hartford: Take I-91 north to State 190 at exit 47 east in Enfield. From Springfield, Massachusetts, take I-91 south to Connecticut State 190 at exit 47 east in Enfield. This trip runs approximately forty-nine miles.

Highlights: Shenipsit State Forest, backcountry small towns, Nipmuck State Forest, Mountain Laurel Sanctuary, Bigelow Hollow State Park.

Enfield to Shenipsit State Forest

This trip gets better and better as you progress. But at the outset you have to drive through a long section of new malls on either side of State 190. The Brookside Plaza on the right with its modern blue-roof motif means you're on the correct track out of town.

Stay on State 190 as you approach a Y junction about a half mile later. State 190 and Hazard Avenue coincide in Hazardville nearly two miles later. In the center of Hazardville the

1869 two-level Hazardville Institute building stands on the left corner where State 192 north crosses State 190; the old intriguing building is listed on the National Register of Historic Places and is currently being refurbished.

In another mile and a half, continue on State 190 as you pass State 191 and finally get more into the country on your way to Somers. As you drive through this northeastern area of Connecticut, keep in mind that this section may have ended up being part of Massachusetts were it not for persistent fuming and hollering about questionable surveys of the state line.

In 1614 the Dutch seafarer Adrien Block first sailed his forty-four-foot *Restless* up the Connecticut River past Hartford to what is believed to have stopped him—the falls at Enfield. This initial European exploration slowly opened the doors to sparse settlement of the area over the decades. Originally, the British charter established the southern side of Massachusetts as running a line due west from a point three miles south of the southernmost point of the Charles River. To establish the boundary officially, in 1642 Massachusetts surveyors figured that laying the line by foot was beyond the call of duty. So they sailed around Cape Cod and up the Connecticut River, as Adrien Block had twenty-eight years earlier, to what they thought was the equivalent latitude of their starting point. It wasn't. It was eight miles too far south, and as a result they sliced away a significant chunk of Connecticut land for Massachusetts's purposes.

Much howling ensued, and Connecticut started its own survey three years later, completing it in 1695. As expected, the Connecticut survey proved unacceptable to Massachusetts. But by this time Connecticut people had settled into the Enfield area on the eastern side of the Connecticut River and Suffield on the western side. More official temper tantrums followed until by 1702 the two colonies agreed that Connecticut should get seven of the eight miles in dispute. Grumpy relations continued, with Connecticut charging that Massachusetts reneged on the deal.

The two disputants then agreed in 1708 to seek solution from a third party—the absentee British in London. After appealing by written documents to London, the colonies realized this could turn against both of them in a catastrophic way by having the British cancel all private colonial charters. Connecticut and Massachusetts reversed direction and hurried instead to solve their own problems. By 1713 the colonies came to a solution: Connecticut would agree that Massachusetts could retain governship of its old southern border towns in exchange for having Massachusetts cede to Connecticut certain western frontier land in Massachusetts and New Hampshire.

How did the people living in the disputed area fare? They howled a lot, especially at the higher Massachusetts taxes, and finally mounted a separatist movement. In 1747 the people of Woodstock, Somers, Enfield (towns on this trip), and Suffield, all at this time within Massachusetts, petitioned the Connecticut General Assembly for inclusion in the Connecticut colony. They were unsuccessful when Connecticut's new leaders tried to open negotiations with Massachusetts, which refused. These four towns had appealed to the original 1662 charter that showed the towns within the Connecticut borders.

Ever determined, Connecticut went ahead anyway without Massachusetts's compliance and voted Woodstock, Enfield, Somers, and Suffield into its colony. At the same time, Connecticut threatened Massachusetts again to take the issue to Britain, but general colonial unrest preoccupied the British and the matter was ignored in London. Massachusetts in turn voted reconfirmation of the four towns—and its taxes—within its own boundaries. Nevertheless, Connecticut continued to govern the towns. By 1800 the fuming and fussing abated, and the four troublesome towns remained in Connecticut.

Far from troublesome now, the drive on State 190 through this area offers you unpretentious backcountry scenes of small working towns between stretches of rolling, wooded terrain etched by long tunnels of trees. By the time you reach Somers about seven miles from Enfield, the feeling of more rural detachment from the urban congestion takes hold. When Somers was first established in its bare bones by Benjamin Jones, it was called "East Enfield." The town and its environs have always looked to agriculture as their base of support, producing potatoes, tobacco, and dairy products. In the nineteenth century bonnetmaking flourished, but as with many "hat cities," this industry faded away.

Continue straight through town on State 190. Once into the woods, you'll notice that here, as in many other places along the way, the woods are young and thin-trunked. The forests have reclaimed much of this land from early clearing for agriculture, which is generally no longer active. Some of this land is preserved as state forests, although this by no means suggests that no trees are cut in these preserves. Often, in fact, state forests are used specifically for supplying timber in controlled allotments.

State forests also offer pleasant detours from the asphalt highways, and the Shenipsit State Forest is one of these. Located about 2.5 miles east of Somers, look for the identification sign on the right. Not much warning is given, but the sign isn't hidden, either. Turn onto Sodom Road and follow it into the forest. You'll pass through some thinned-out woodlands and a gravel pit not sheltered enough from the road. But generally this makes an easygoing side trip under the cool canopy.

In six-tenths of a mile, Lucay Road veers to the left. Keep straight and wind through the quiet woods. The earthen road is well graded and easy to maneuver.

In 1.8 miles, the road bends around and down slightly to a small pond. With a single picnic table overlooking the pond, this makes a secluded lunch spot that is surely off the beaten path. Probably the only other visitors you'll have will be friendly birds.

Stafford Springs to Mountain Laurel Sanctuary

Once you are back on State 190, continue east uphill past the surprisingly large Johnson Memorial Medical Center on the left and then downhill two miles to West Stafford and the State 30 junction on the right; the Second Congregational Church stands on the left. If a rummage and food sale here meet your schedule, stop in and have a look. Sometimes these affairs produce unexpected creations for the eye and taste buds. And the price is often right in these small communities.

Actually, rummage sales, flea markets, and tag sales have a long, playful history in New England. When long-hoarded attic goods are uncovered and brought to light, all sorts of possibilities loom for the discerning eye. Granted, the gem of a Grandma Moses painting might sprout before you only after rummaging through interminable layers of chipped teacups and dented pewter mugs—but that's the fun of it all.

As for food sales, sometimes these too make good offerings for the road. Instead of steam-table hamburgers, you might latch on to an aromatic loaf of fresh anadama bread, shiny sticky orange buns, or a warm fresh pie made with Northern Spy apples and real maple syrup, served with a generous slice of Vermont cheddar cheese. You never know what will turn up at a church food sale or Sunday supper, but you do know it won't be manufactured food from a fast-food station. Road food can be good, if you get out of the chain-store habit on these back byways.

Speaking of the unexpected, in the next few miles some surprises await. Two miles from the State 30 turnoff, Joanne's

Gourmet Coffee & Bakery shop on the right stocks choice coffees for the road. Another mile after you pass the small charming Stafford park and gazebo on the left, Chez Pierre French restaurant resides in a disarmingly attractive reconstructed house on the left.

Then two-tenths of a mile farther, be on the lookout for La Petite France, a French bakery. A small sign hangs outside the blue-painted house on the right. The exterior is modest indeed and announces little of the grandeur that is French bread and pastry baking. You can park in an adjacent small lot. Inside, the offerings are clearly in the European bakery style and taste. In this petite bakery, the glass case displays flaky puff-paste pastries glistening with fruit-coated sauces and filled with apricots, peaches, apples, or blueberries; combinations of raspberry and cheese; croissants; cheese-only pastries; brioche loaves; baguettes; and other crusty French breads. Directly to the rear in plain view are the ovens and preparation tables, maybe even one of the family members slicing fresh strawberries. This is not your franchised doughnut shop or supermarket "bakery" where more likely than not the doughs are manufactured in some other state and merely ovened on the premises. This instead is where owner Colette Berube bakes from scratch and makes sure La Petite France carries on the "real bakery" tradition. Here you'll wish your own neighborhood had such a shop.

Another half mile downhill takes you straight through the main street of Stafford Springs, its low, two-story brick buildings lining both sides of the street. On the left the Haymarket Common shows what a small town with little working space can do. This is an inviting town-center park on the side of a hill lined with fine stonework, well-situated trees, and stone platforms, all mixing to create a sense of calm and restfulness.

As you proceed down this short street, the old railroad station and tracks curve through town on the right. Straight ahead the Warren Memorial Town Hall, built in 1922, commands the scene. The town grew from the attraction of nearby sulfur and iron mineral springs, which brought the local

A gazebo on the town green in Stafford Springs

Mohegans, Nipmucks, and other Native Americans. The curative properties of the waters, which made them "lively," as it was described then, were known widely among the natives, who pitched their wigwams around the spring for weeks to drink and bathe in the magical stuff. An old Indian trail, known later as the Nipmuck Trail, was used by the Nipmucks for their annual pilgrimage south to the ocean shoreline for shell fishing. In return the Pequots and Mohegans trekked the trails north for shad and salmon fishing.

Word spread of these famous springs all the way to Quincy, outside Boston, from where the once and future President John Adams in 1771 journeyed for health's sake. Adams was only the most notable tip of the elite who visited Stafford Springs (originally called Medicine Springs and Indian Springs), ostensibly for his health but no doubt mostly for rest and recreation in these undulating, peaceful hills.

Settled by whites in 1719, Stafford and Stafford Springs, where the brooks and streams meet, used their hydropower for iron-ore furnaces and textile manufacturing. The town was named after Staffordshire, in England, although Stafford Springs took its name from the mineral springs, becoming the most famous of the mineral springs in the new nation.

In 1802 Dr. Samuel Willard built part of the old Stafford Springs House hotel; ownership passed through several hands during the nineteenth century and into the next, when it was destroyed by fire in 1959.

As you head straight for the town hall, follow State 190 when it makes a left and then a quick right past the U.S. Post Office. Proceed uphill and out of Stafford Springs as you drive into the country. Marshes now and then appear by the side of the road. Soon the Union town line appears. Then three-quarters of a mile later a sign on the right indicates the Nipmuck State Forest access road. At this point you might like another cruising forest drive over a dirt road, and if so turn right here. At eight-tenths of a mile into the forest, veer left onto the main road as you drive deeper through this thinned-out woodland. The road rolls softly over the terrain and is a pleasant diversion, but after about two miles you still won't find a pond or brook, as you did earlier in the Shenipsit State Forest.

On the other hand, 1.1 miles farther east on State 190 you'll come to another entrance to the Nipmuck State Forest. This time it's for the Mountain Laurel Sanctuary, well worth visiting, especially during the blooming spring and early summer seasons. This evergreen shrub is native to the eastern United States and, in fact, it is the state flower of Connecticut. The white and pink blossoms appear on the ends of the branches, sometimes almost covering the shrub with their glories.

The sanctuary is well maintained, and the entire drive into it covers less than a mile. At the half-mile point, the mountain laurel grow bigger and thicker. A picnic table sits back here on the right. A few isolated white birch trees stand tall above the greenery. Two-tenths of a mile later a bench on the left and another a little later sit in two of the several grassy "coves" by the road for getting out of the car and relaxing a while.

Union to North Woodstock

Back on State 190 east, continue straight past the I-84 west right turn two-tenths of a mile later. In 1.3 miles more go happily over the I-84 bridge and continue deeper into relaxing country with mountain laurel everywhere. When you crest a small hill about another 2.25 miles later, the lilliputian town center of Union appears. This crossroads town shows its simple heart of white church, 1910 public library, war memorial green, and 1850 house on the hill for all passersby to take home in picturesque memory.

Because of the rough terrain and soil, Union was the last town east of the Connecticut River to take root. But back in 1633 John Oldham of Massachusetts discovered through the local natives that black lead or graphite was relatively abundant here. This paid off, because during the Revolutionary War it was used by cannon foundries. The earliest settlers moved here permanently in 1727. Thirty years later Union had 500 people, curiously, about the same as the population today. Although the numbers haven't changed much over the centuries, the nineteenth-century industries of making shoes and ax handles have changed to the agriculture and forestry of today.

In three-tenths of a mile uphill turn right at State 171 at the sign for State 197 and Bigelow Hollow State Park. In about 1.25 miles of hilly driving, suddenly you dip into the bottom of a hollow with Bigelow Brook, looking like a long, narrow lake, on your left. The entrance to the park is a short distance on the left as you ascend the other side.

For the next mile down this paved access road, picnic tables are scattered in designated areas to the left in the trees. These spots are located next to the brook and are inviting places to spend some time.

A slightly more open area is found at the end of this road. First you come to a parking lot and a boat-launching area sloping gently to the water's edge. This inlet, narrow and pristine looking, is lined to the shore with tall evergreens at the edge of a gray granite basin. To the left of the launch beach, a wide path leads to a picnic area on a point. It's less than 300 yards away, a pleasant walk through trees and mountain laurel. Tables are available under the protection of pines that whisper in the breeze. The brook curves around the miniature peninsula, making the combination of blue water, green pines, and hilly silhouettes of the islands and shoreline medicine enough to mellow out anybody anywhere.

On the way back to the park entrance, you can stop along some of the paths to the shore, if you haven't already done so. This is a calming park and a fitting balance to the frenetic scene of the Enfield malls at the outset of the trip.

The last eight miles to North Woodstock take you through equally reassuring countryside. From the Bigelow State Park entrance, turn left back onto State 197 and remain on it the rest of the way. At a Y junction a mile later, take State 197, not State 171. At 1.8 miles the Woodstock town line appears, and you're in hilly and winding but good back-country—some horses in their fields, marshes and dense woods on either side of the road, plentiful mountain laurel along the way.

Weathered old barns with stout cupolas remain from more active years, now a bit forlorn in the wooded hills. A mile after the State 171 junction, State 198 crosses at a stop sign; proceed straight on State 197 east. Two miles later on this tree-hugging road, some cleared fields open up the scene, then the woods engulf you again until you're cruising down onto a final stretch of flatland before the stop sign in the heart of North Woodstock.

In the Area

Chez Pierre (West Stafford): 203-684-5826

Joanne's Gourmet Coffee & Bakery (West Stafford):
203-684-5854

La Petite France (Stafford Springs): 203-684-9408

Stafford Chamber of Commerce (Stafford Springs):
203-684-6568

6 ~

Voluntown
to Mystic

From **Worcester, Massachusetts:** Take I-290 south to I-395
south to exit 85 east and then
State 138 to Voluntown. From
Hartford take State 2 south to
I-395 north at Norwich to exit
85 and State 138 east to Voluntown. This trip runs approximately forty-five miles.

Highlights: Green Falls Pond
and State Forest, rural homes,
farm fields, Old Mystic village
center, The Indian and Colonial Research Center, seacoast
and harbors, Old Lighthouse
Museum, Stonington war
site, seventeenth- and eighteenth-century homes, Mystic
Seaport Maritime Museum,
Mystic Marinelife Aquarium.

Voluntown to North Stonington

This trip covers a wide breadth of territory in a relatively short
distance. You'll be traveling through an intriguing variety of
sights and sounds: state forests and craggy seacoast, small-
town centers and big-city outskirts. The deep woodlands
you'll cruise through going straight south by the Rhode Island
border lead to the salt-air openness of the coves and inlets on
the Atlantic shoreline.

Begin at Voluntown, a small community in the center of the five major sections of the Pachaug State Forest, which covers a large area north and south of the town. The name Voluntown derives from an interesting history. Volunteers who had fought in the Narragansett War of 1675–1676 requested and were granted land for their effort when in October 1696 Lt. Thomas Leffingwell of Norwich and Sergeant John Frink of Stonington petitioned the General Court "that they with the rest of the English volunteers in the former wars might have a plantation granted them." A tract of land six miles square was indeed granted, which is now the present towns of Voluntown and Sterling. In 1708 the plantation was called "Volluntown," obviously named after the volunteering men who fought in the war.

This history is celebrated in a small triangle of land where State 138 and State 49 meet. Follow State 49 south. You'll see clearly enough how State 49 takes two quick turns into nice woods with scattered homes along the two-lane road. The byway climbs steadily at a slight angle for a little more than a mile before narrowing. A half mile later open sky appears on the left—it's a commercial sand and gravel pit that sounds worse than it really is.

At this point be on the lookout (three-tenths of a mile after the beginning of the gravel pit) for a small "Green Falls" sign on the left. The sign is lettered in yellow on a brown-painted post. Turn onto this earthen road and drive slowly into the Green Falls section of the Pachaug State Forest. Along the way you'll spot many fieldstone foundations and walls, remnants of early-day farmhouses and small barns and hardscrabble fields. The woods and underbrush are relatively young growth hiding these stone wall legacies, but you'll see some just the same.

A mile from the entrance the road curves to the right at a sharp angle and takes you to a kiosk at a junction with another road entering the area. Remain on this road through mostly level-land conifers and airy woods for a little more than 1.5 miles where Green Falls Pond comes into view, a pleasant surprise in the deep forest.

The road here curves downward two-tenths of a mile to a boat-launch area. Next to this a short distance farther is a flat area at water level. Here in this small, quiet space you'll find room to park your car, picnic tables, outhouses, fire pits, and—a tenth of a mile more to the end of the road—a trailhead. At this point too the lake tightens to a nib where you can see an enchanting long view of the pond lined with pines.

With its island of gray granite boulders and healthy trees, modest-sized Green Falls Pond evokes a charming invitation to linger a while and enjoy the repose. Several other vantage points where the broad-shouldered boulders dominate the shoreline give you seats to sit, breathe deeply, and relax.

Return the same way to State 49. The next long stretch takes you past isolated rural scenes that will appeal to anyone's sense of cozy country living. The meandering miles of woodlands now and then are interrupted with enclaves of tailored rural homes and comforting farm fields. For instance, about a mile after you get back on State 49 south, after climbing the terrain, you emerge onto a long stretch of farm fields, many of which are encircled by an unusually high, loose, thin stone wall. A sawmill operates on the right.

Then down into the trees you go again (if it's early spring dogwood tree blossoms float their white and pink petal clusters against the dark backdrop of leafless branches). Three-quarters of a mile later the road dips to a small cement bridge built in 1929 over Koistiner Brook, and just beyond this a simple but lustrous scene of stone walls, a dammed pond, and farm horses in fenced fields will surely capture your attention. Be on the watch here for an unusual stone outbuilding on the left, too.

Soon the North Stonington town line appears and with it come more stone walls. The walls are a clue to the harsh farm life the land created for the early settlers and a reason many left for the West, where good planting soil didn't require the backbreaking labor of harvesting the boulders before putting in the potatoes. The stone walls did indeed come from the stone fields.

After passing the First Baptist Church, which stands alone on a hill on the right, State 49 declines for the next three miles. Then comes a stop sign three-quarters of a mile later; turn right onto State 49 and continue following the yellow line for about two miles until you reach State 184.

Old Mystic to the Seacoast

From the junction with State 49, turn right onto State 184, which is a step up from byway to highway. Continue on State 184 toward Old Mystic, but before you get there a pleasant detour comes up soon.

In nine-tenths of a mile State 184 takes you to a rotary, the Eastern Seaboard version of Russian roulette. Fortunately, the danger level of this rotary ranks well below that of the terror circles of Boston. As you approach and curve around the rotary, bear left and then right, remaining on State 184. A half mile later on the left, a sign points you to Adam's Garden of Eden of flowers and herbs. Drive down Anguilla Road one mile where on the left the entrance opens onto a spread of earthly delights to wander through and maybe buy for the road.

Open April through Christmas (and closed Tuesdays), this garden displays herbs, everlastings, scented geraniums, seasonal decorations, mums, and pumpkins in the fall. A country shop offers two stories of wreaths, hanging pots, books, table displays, dried flower arrangements, and many other items.

*Adam's Garden of Eden, one of Connecticut's many
nurseries and garden centers*

The field next to the entrance sports an unusual feature—
dig-your-own chrysanthemums. The principle operates the
same as pick-your-own strawberries and apples. One of Ed
Adam's favorite sights was seeing a New York woman in
fashionable country attire kick off her high-heel shoes and
squirm her feet into the soil while she dug her own mums,
enjoying every moment of a brief but exhilarating immersion
into country life.

He tells too of the time when a woman on a jet liner in a
landing-approach pattern saw in the middle of all the green

woodlands below a patch of reds and yellows and blues. After landing she made arrangements to search out this brilliant-looking island of colors, which, of course, was Adam's Garden of Eden. She drove back and forth along the country road network for hours—and found it.

In front of the country shop, a buckboard-style, wood-sided wagon on big iron spoke wheels stands filled with flowers. Next to the shop are a white garden trellis and gazebo. Behind the shop paths lead to garden displays for visitors to roam at will. Most of the stock is raised on the ten-acre grounds. Two acres are devoted to raising pumpkins; a section is set aside for cut-your-own Christmas trees. Says Ed: "We do a little bit of everything."

After returning to State 184, turn left and proceed west past the Stonington town line 1.5 miles later. In another quarter mile, the Pequot Plant Farm on the left has been on this side road since 1969 (it's only a quarter mile on the right off State 184). This large, efficient farm allows a walk through the greenhouses and grounds.

Continue west on State 184, passing State 201 two miles later as it enters on the right. Then 1.2 miles later on this easy driving road you'll cross the Groton line, and 1.2 miles more turn left at the light to Old Mystic on State 27. In two-tenths of a mile this road takes you quickly to the village center.

The compact village is little more than a curve in the road, but what it contains is worth seeing up close. To the left as you enter the center you'll see the Old Mystic Inn on Main Street and the Old Mystic Country Store (very much updated with photocopying machine and other marvels of the modern world). To the right stands the Old Mystic Methodist Church with its Greek Revival white pillars across the street from the Indian & Colonial Research Center. Stop in at this research library/museum housed in an 1856 red-brick bank building on

Main Street. Displays of Native American artifacts, photographs from 1895–1917, manuscripts from the early eighteenth century, and rare books on Indians of the area are shown to enlighten and fascinate.

From the Old Mystic town center, drive straight through Main Street for about two-tenths of a mile to State 234 east on the left. Follow this route uphill a short distance where a blue sign instructs you that this is a "Scenic Road." The road is pleasant enough, but it appears that the sign and designation applied before the scattered homes-in-the-woods were built on this ridgetop.

Nevertheless, this way takes you through rural residential scenes for nearly three miles, and in itself it's restful and interesting. After driving by the Pequot Golf Course and over I-95, in four-tenths of a mile back into the woods, turn right on the first back road at a three-way junction with signs to US 1 and intriguing Stonington.

Stonington

In 1.5 miles proceed straight across US 1 at the signal light with the directional sign to Stonington village. In a quarter mile on the right some of the seacoast inlet system shimmers through the trees, with another good view on the right in another quarter mile. At the stop sign, turn left and curve around to another stop sign a short distance away. Turn right and drive over the new bridge and curve left into the main section of Stonington.

You're on Water Street now. Drive slowly down the narrow road (you won't be able to go any other speed) to the end one mile away. The narrowness of Water Street evokes the era of small-scale living in colonial, revolutionary, early-eighteenth-century seacoast towns. The buildings press tight against one another. After you pass the Stonington Public

Library on the left, the buildings that line both sides of the street are filled now with goods mostly for visitors—art, specialty foods, hand-crafted clothing. It's a good place to stroll, if you're lucky enough to find a parking spot off the beaten street.

One-way Water Street leads you directly to the seacoast point. Immediately before you drive onto the parking lot point surrounded on three sides by the Atlantic, the Old Lighthouse Museum catches your eye on the left. This squat, granite-block, 1823 lighthouse was the first government-operated light in the state. The outside is surrounded by a white picket fence and lawn. Inside, the museum shows you all sorts of ancient mariner lore and artifacts, including whaling gear and goods from the Orient brought back by traders and explorers.

At the point, where the once-ragged edge of the coastline has been transformed into valuable harbors and inlets, a small, unobtrusive memorial signifies an important contribution to the making of the nation: "This is to remember. The brave men of Stonington defeated a landing force from British ship *Ramillies* bent on burning the town and its shipping. August 10, 1814."

Being located so close to Rhode Island, Stonington faced border trouble periodically, including fighting the "confiscation" of taxes by Rhode Island agents when the state line fluctuated here and there in colonial days. More than one of these agents were arrested. Connecticut became one of the most densely populated of the colonies, and Stonington grew rapidly, too. The town increased 54 percent in population to 5,412 residents in a twenty-year span by 1774. In that year Stonington claimed the largest number of Indians (237) of all the Connecticut towns. The town also had 219 Negro slaves. A year later forty men were assigned and paid by the Patriots to protect Stonington, as indeed others were stationed at exposed villages along Long Island Sound.

Then came August 9, 1814, when a small British fleet, commanded by Captain Thomas M. Hardy, appeared offshore. He sent this message to the people of Stonington: "Not wishing to destroy the unoffending inhabitants residing in the town of Stonington, one hour is given them from the receipt of this to move out of town." Oh, yeah?

The townspeople had only two eighteen-pounders and one four-pounder cannon mounted on a small earthwork. Quickly, they burned smoky tar barrels to summon Colonel William Randall's regiment of militia, who pushed back the British landing forces on August 9 and 10. In return, the British bombarded Stonington for the next three days from their five ships. Stonington resident Amos Palmer reported that the British shot at least sixty tons of metal into the village but wounded only one man. British casualties totaled several score; the warship *Despatch* was seriously damaged. Later, Philip Freneau's ballad on the Battle of Stonington contained these lines: "It cost the king ten thousand pounds/To have a dash at Stonington."

For a few years after the smoke cleared, Stonington joined the rush for whaling in 1822. By 1837 a railroad line connected Providence to Stonington, which changed the coastal point village drastically. When a boat line connected with the railroad line, industry thrived, belching out noise and smoke of a different kind.

Stonington today has many intriguing sites to see and ponder. This is a compact, walkers' town. Up close you can see some of the mansions that displayed the wealth from a profitable era of shipbuilding, sealing, and whaling. You can walk over original cobblestones, granite blocks interspaced on the streets with flagstones to secure underfooting. Cottages of ropemakers and jewelers with elaborate wrought-iron gates and fencing, mansions of shipowners, houses where artists James Whistler and poet Stephen Vincent Benét lived are worth searching out. A brochure of a walking trip through town is available at the public library, the lighthouse museum, and other locations.

If you wish to move on, however, drive from the lighthouse point back on Water Street a quarter mile and turn right (you have to turn because Water Street becomes a one-way road) at a small memorial park with two cannons. Turn left on Main Street as you proceed around the park, and keep on the lookout for some of these old sites along the way. The Customs House of 1827 on your left stands out for its granite base and four Greek Revival columns. Look for Wall Street near here and turn right for a quarter-mile drive past a row of houses. At the end you emerge onto an open area with parking available for a few cars, giving you a view of the rocky coastline.

Return to Main Street, turn right, and continue until you arrive a short distance later at the town green, the public library, and post office. Follow the signs for I-95 and US 1, which take you in a couple quick turns back to the start of Water Street. Return the way you came over the bridge, left at the I-95 sign, curve around a little as you enter—but this time continue straight for US 1A and "to US 1." (In other words, do not turn on North Main Street toward I-95.) At the end of the block you'll see the US 1A sign. Turn right and in three-tenths of a mile cross a short bridge over an inlet. In another half mile you'll reach US 1 at a signal light.

Mystic Seaport and Aquarium

Once on US 1 heading toward Mystic, in about 1.5 miles a detour to Lords Point comes up on the left. This is a residential area of a mixed array of old and new houses, interesting but unspectacular. In three-tenths of a mile after US 1, turn left after a curve and steer straight to the end. Then circle left and you'll quickly find a pier to your right over the water. Lords Point makes a nice enough diversion and gives you another angle of the shoreline.

71

Return to US 1 and turn left toward Mystic again, which
you'll reach in about five miles. Just before you enter downtown Mystic, turn right at the I-95 directional sign onto State
27 north. This takes you a short distance to the Mystic Seaport
Maritime Museum.

Stonington and Mystic, small settlements as they were,
produced two of the most important and prosperous industries of the early nineteenth century—shipbuilding and whaling. Mystic especially was favored with wide, calm water sites
on the Mystic River for building the seafaring tall ships. After
the War of 1812, the revival of whaling and sealing energized
the shipbuilding business, and as the nation grew more
wealthy and demanded better products, the Mystic ship-
builders and shipowners grew wealthy and were in demand.
Many packets, sloops, and clipper ships were built at Mystic,
some of them making the difficult 110-day voyage to San
Francisco around the unpredictably dangerous southern tip of
South America, where the cold currents and winds near the
Antarctic clashed.

After Boston, Mystic became the largest New England
shipping port from a burgeoning demand for supplies to support the Civil War. Mystic shipyards produced fifty-six steam-
ers (some 230 feet long) for the federal navy.

Over the years the pursuit of whale oil and whale bone
generated increasing production of ships, especially for hunt-
ing the valuable sperm whale in deep waters. Mystic sent its
first whaling ship, the *Aeronaut,* in 1832, to the South Atlantic,
and many more after this. As the national population grew so
did the public call for whale-oil illumination and lubrication.
Spermaceti candles were sought and bought by the wealthy,
and whale bone was used in corsets, stays, and umbrella ribs.

Early whalers were mostly New England Yankees, but
after the 1830s Indians, Portuguese, Negroes, mulattoes,
South Sea Islanders, and western Europeans joined the
crews. Later, criminals, drifters, and adventurers became part

The Charles W. Morgan *at Mystic*

of the rugged voyages, resulting in increasingly rough life and less efficiency. All crew members were paid by percentages. A captain might earn 1/10 of the total net profit returns of a voyage, mates 1/38, ordinary seamen and cooks 1/100, the "green" hands as little as 1/200. If the voyages brought back little to process and sell, the crew received little, sometimes owing money and thus being forced to sign on for the next voyage to pay off debts.

When petroleum was discovered in the mid-nineteenth century, it quickly replaced whale oil as the choice for illumination. The era of deep-sea whaling died out, but not before Mystic ranked third in Connecticut whaling ports by sending out 105 voyages between 1832 and 1860.

Mystic Seaport captures some of this historic, fascinating life. The seventeen-acre museum winds around the water's edge where tall ships are docked for boarding and up-close examination. The centerpiece whaleship *Charles W. Morgan*, built in 1841 and 113 feet long, is the only surviving wooden whaleship in the nation; it's docked as part of the museum. The *L. A. Dunton* fishing schooner, the *Joseph Conrad* training ship, and the S. S. *Sabina* are all on the museum water.

Two shipbuilding yards from 1837 and 1851 once occupied the site of the museum, which was established in 1929. All sorts of shops line the shore: maritime commercial buildings, old houses, food shops, a bank, and a schoolhouse all represent a historic waterfront village. Skilled boatbuilders and wood-carvers demonstrate old-time talents.

Continuing north up State 27 about a half mile takes you to the intersection with I-95. Turn right at the signal here onto Coogan Boulevard and follow the signs for the Mystic Marinelife Aquarium about a half mile later.

Surrounded by a complex of tourist-style shops, the aquarium makes a pleasant end to the trip. All sorts of exotic fish are displayed in this large sea zoo. Huge tanks of sharks and demonstration theaters for whales and dolphins are especially popular. Separate outdoor exhibits for penguins (eighteen different species) and for seals from New England, California, and the Pribilof Islands of Alaska add to an enjoyable end of the road.

In the Area

Adam's Garden of Eden (Pawcatuck): 203-536-2820

Indian and Colonial Research Center (Old Mystic):
203-536-9771

Mystic Marinelife Aquarium (Mystic): 203-536-3323,
203-536-9631

Mystic Seaport Maritime Museum (Mystic): 203-572-0711

Old Lighthouse Museum (Stonington Village): 203-535-1440
Old Mystic Country Store (Old Mystic): 203-536-3946
Old Mystic Inn (Old Mystic): 203-572-9422
Pequot Golf Course (Stonington): 203-535-1898
Pequot Plant Farm (Old Mystic): 203-535-1785
Stonington Public Library (Stonington): 203-535-0658

7 ~

Higganum
to Old
Saybrook

From Hartford: Take I-91 south to State 9 south through Middletown to exit 10 and State 154. This trip runs approximately seventy-eight miles.

Highlights: Haddam Meadows State Park, Goodspeed Opera House, the Connecticut River, Gillette Castle State Park, rural towns, coastal views, Old Saybrook, Saybrook Point marina, Castle Inn.

Higganum to Haddam

Something always new and different lies around the next bend on this trip—300-year-old towns, yacht marinas, stone castles, riverboats, an opera house. The excursion begins in rural woods, ends on the oceanfront, and in between some easy backcountry driving gives you a sense of getting away from it all.

Begin on State 154 south as you turn off State 9 at exit 10. In three-tenths of a mile you cross Bible Rock Brook, a small stream that goes under the road and is a clue that you're on the right track. A half mile later an enclave of houses appears in this wooded section. In less than another mile you cross the Higganum town line and soon dip down through the community center. This small cluster of buildings portends that the future miles of this trip are indeed far away from the hustle and bustle of speedy State 9, a major highway to and from Middletown. Leave it all behind and cruise yourself into country slowdown.

Two miles later, after passing among trees that seem to wrap around you, flash-by, blue-water scenes of the Connecticut River sparkle through the woods on the left. Then a mile later, only about 4.5 miles from the outset of the trip, the Haddam Meadows State Park entrance on the left comes up quickly. Turn in here for a shoreside visit to the great wide river.

The 147-acre park is noted for its giant playing fields at the bottom of a short entrance ramp. Follow the dirt road to the right, veering right again at the junction and steering straight for another half mile to the end, where the road circles at the shoreline. A few picnic tables are available here for a lunch or snack by the Connecticut River that flows inexorably into the Atlantic.

The park has several boat-launching areas, the main one asphalted, a couple others off the return loop road alongside the shoreline brush and trees. It also offers direct views of the domed Haddam Connecticut Yankee Nuclear Power Plant straight across the river on the east shore. The quarter-century-old plant contributes more than half the tax base for the town of Haddam. But the nuclear machinery is scheduled for decommissioning in the next decade, and citizens of Haddam are tilting with what to do for the future of their town.

Once back on State 154 (Middlesex Turnpike), the Haddam town center is only a quarter mile uphill. A clutterless, open-feeling town, Haddam shows its 300-year-old history well. In 1660 the General Court of the British colonial powers received a petition of "Several members of this Collony presenting their desires unto this Court of setling a plantation at 30 Mile Island." A committee to view the land was appointed and reported back favorably. In 1662 two women named Sepunnemoe and Towkishki, with Turramuggus and his son Unlaus and others of the Wangunk Tribe, sold land to the Connecticut Colony. In 1668 this land and town were incorporated and boundaries were established from "Ye Greate River" westward into the wilderness six miles, and from "Ye Greate River" eastward six miles into the wilderness.

Some of the history through the generations is displayed in the three-story, gambrel-roofed Thankful Arnold House located off Wakley Hill Road to the right as you enter the town center. This is the headquarters of the Haddam Historical Society, a 1794 house restored by Mr. and Mrs. Isaac Arnold and dedicated to its purpose in 1965. It contains period furnishings and a garden of flowers, herbs, and vegetables found in the late eighteenth and early nineteenth centuries.

Today Haddam, named for a town in Hertfordshire, England, counts about 7,000 residents who work at the atomic energy plant, lumberyards, marinas along the river, and in plants manufacturing tools, wire products, and agricultural machinery. As the original plantation boundaries state, the town straddles Ye Greate River, whose eastern side you'll visit soon. The serious economic threat brought on by the inevitable decommissioning of the nuclear power plant counters its long-stable yesteryears. As a scenic location on the river, Haddam prospered from a busy network of early transportation routes. Shipbuilding, commercial wharves, warehouses, and a thriving mercantile economy turned the town into a prosperous community. The hilly country here that feeds rivers and brooks into the Connecticut River also provided power for mills and factories. Steamboats, ferries, the construction of the Middlesex Turnpike at the turn of the nineteenth century, a railroad, and the Industrial Revolution in general brought economic stimulation throughout the nineteenth century.

Keep this in mind as you drive through the nice and easy town toward Tylerville about three miles south on State 154, where you'll cross Ye Greate River, which provided so much to Haddam in the past.

East Haddam to Gillette Castle State Park

In Tylerville at the highway junction, turn left onto State 82 toward East Haddam across the Connecticut River. But in a half mile before you reach the bridge, a right turn at the sign takes you down to a sprawling complex of parking lot, ticket office, and restaurant of Camelot Cruises. Here cruise ships seating 500 passengers depart on 2.5-hour trips down the lower Connecticut River en route to Old Saybrook past Gillette Castle. Some cruises have murder-mystery plays acted on board; others can be reserved for weddings and special occasions.

Back onto State 82 and across the river you go. As you approach East Haddam on the high eastern rivershore, the Goodspeed Opera House looms its four-story, turreted bulk immediately after you finish the bridge. This rejuvenated show palace carries on the high-prancing tradition of light musical comedies. First built in 1876 by shipping and banking magnate William H. Goodspeed, who was also a theater fan, the opera house enjoyed the bubbling activity of both a theater and a professional office building before subsequent years of deterioration.

At one point the building was a storage depot for the state highway department, and then it was marked for demolition in 1958. The following year the Goodspeed Opera House Foundation was established by local preservationists, and work to restore and reactivate the theater began in earnest. By 1963 the opera house was fully revived as a musical theater,

Enjoy a musical comedy at the
Goodspeed Opera House in Haddam

celebrating its rededication on June 18, 1963, with the production *Oh Lady! Lady!!*

The opera house shows off all the accoutrements of a lush bygone era. As you enter, the grand staircase leads its curved, marbleized balustrade and fire-engine red carpet up the center, branching to both sides toward the 360-seat auditorium (with the original drop curtain depicting the "State of New York"). The Green Room on the second level elegantly displays velveteen chairs and draping curtains, in tones of green, of course. Downstairs, the Victorian Bar, overlooking the great river, winds its polished walnut bar and brass rail in an elongated S in a room of English flocked wallpaper. To one side of the bar a door opens to the Ladies' Drinking Parlor, a cozy, out-of-sight room decorated in mid-nineteenth-century French wallpaper—because in those pristine days ladies simply didn't, or weren't allowed to, drink in public with the gentlemen.

From the opera house, continue on State 82 past the East Haddam town office across the street and curve left toward the woods, then veer right a short way later, keeping on State 82. For the next 1.5 miles you'll drive up the terrain through pleasant woods and cross Succor Brook twice before coming to a stop sign. Turn right here, staying on State 82, and in short order veer right toward Gillette State Park, about one mile along a nice road. Another 1.5 miles or so a narrow byway takes you to the park entrance.

The six-tenths-of-a-mile-long entrance road shows you what a gem of a park this is. Not far in, the "Castle Oak" on the left grows in white oak sturdiness by the side of the road—it boasts a 17-foot girth, a 94-foot height, and a 128-foot spread. Then the entrance road ahead passes a cultivated pond with an arched stone bridge at the far end. A little farther on you'll see wooden-walk bridges over marshes and gullies. Footpaths lead off into the woods here and there.

The main attraction is the fieldstone showplace home of William Gillette, who died in 1937 after a career as a well-known actor playing Sherlock Holmes. The porches and patios of the castle overlook the Connecticut River from a wonderful, high vantage point, the river far and away below flowing gently to the south.

Gillette knew the value of his 122-acre estate. His will states that his executors must "see to it that the property did not fall into the hands of some blithering saphead who has no conception of where he is or with what surrounded." Fortunately, the state of Connecticut purchased the estate in 1943 so that now the twenty-four-room castle and woodlands are maintained as a state park for present and future country-road travelers to enjoy.

Up close and inside, you'll see that Gillette built the castle of local fieldstone and southern white oak. From 1914 to 1919, twenty men worked on its construction at a cost of more than $1 million. The granite walls stand three to four feet thick at the base of this medieval-style mansion. The interior trim is hand-hewn oak, including the forty-seven doors. Bedroom furniture is built into the structural frame of the castle; some of the other furniture slides on metal tracks. Javanese raffia mats decorate the walls and were made to Gillette's specifications.

The park is ideal for strolling, and if your arrival coincides with a lunch break—perfect. The castle tour and refreshment stand are open during the summer months.

Hadlyme to Old Lyme

As you leave the park grounds, turn right toward narrow State 148 and follow the double yellow line for eight-tenths of a mile to a stop sign. If you turn right, in short order you'll reach an auto ferry across the Connecticut River from Hadlyme to Chester on the western side of the river. The Chester-

Hadlyme Ferry originated in 1769 and remains one of the oldest continuously operating ferries in the country. This gives you a down-by-the-river view.

But to continue ahead, turn left at the stop sign onto the same State 148 east for the start of a soothing rural ride to Old Lyme. First, in a little more than a mile you ride alongside a mysterious backwater swamp with water flower blooms sometimes dotting the murk, with swamp grasses and water birds adding to the intrigue. A half mile later Hadlyme, a small charmer, appears on the scene of this tree-hugging road.

After another half mile you'll come to a stop-sign junction; continue straight on State 82. In about 3.25 miles State 156 south to Old Lyme comes in; take a right and follow this uneventful (and therefore good) road south. Horse farms and horse-show fields line the road here and there.

By the time you reach North Lyme about 2.25 miles later, you're in well-tended rural country. Lyme was first settled in 1664 after a plantation petition was approved. The short story of Lyme goes like this: A "Loving Parting" between Saybrook and East Saybrook signed in 1665 set up Lyme as a separate community of an area unclaimed by either Saybrook, thereby establishing Lyme by default, sort of. During this era, the population everywhere was sparse indeed. In 1667, for instance, thirty families comprised East Saybrook when Lyme was named.

From Lyme, which you'll pass through quickly, the driving remains easy and unhurried. In less than two miles you cross the Hamburg town line. A mile later on the right Tiffany Farm, mostly dairy, gives you a brief open, high-country feeling. Less than a half mile later comes the entrance to Nehantic State Forest on the left. You might like this detour as a diversion into seclusion. The entrance road, although paved, is sometimes bumpy. In 1.2 miles veer to the right toward Uncam Pond, which is another four-tenths of a mile. The road leads to a boat-launch site on a small pond; a few houses spot the woods on the far side. No tables are available.

Once back to State 156, turn left toward the Old Lyme town line 1.6 miles later, where at the Lord Creek Farm you might see a horse and rider practicing jumps. A mile and a half later on the right hints of the seashore suddenly glint through the trees. Old Lyme Marina harbors small sailing boats and yachts.

Less than a half mile later a signal light and I-95 stop you. At this point you could turn onto I-95 west and head the short distance over the Connecticut River to Old Saybrook. Or before doing this you can continue to explore a small section of the Old Lyme side of the river mouth that spills into Long Island Sound and the Atlantic.

To stay on the Old Lyme side a while, steer straight under I-95. Several crossroads lead to shore points along here, where soon shore grass tall and spindly bends in the wind. Two miles from the interstate, a dead-end road on the right called Smith Neck Road takes you to a boat-launching area as part of "Great Island." You'll end up at an inlet with sea grass, sandy edges of an inlet, a lighthouse across the expanse, and other flat and open shoreline views so richly different from the woodlands only a few miles back.

Once back on State 156, drive 1.2 miles to Old Shore Road on the right. In three-tenths of a mile on the right, don't miss a long open field, with a lone hefty maple in the center. In another three-tenths of a mile, turn right onto Brighten Road. In four-tenths of a mile you'll reach the ocean shoreline and a nice long view of Long Island Sound.

Return to Old Shore Road, turn right, and in three-tenths of a mile turn right onto State 156 again. When you reach the town center of Sounds View, about a mile later, you can get to a rather large public beach by turning right in the town center on either Swamm Road or Hartford Avenue. This is a home-town family beach with no fancy tourist stores and knick-knack shops, but the sand is warm and the water blue.

Back on State 156 you'll hit the South Lyme town line a mile later, and before long up comes the access left turn to I-95. Take I-95 south back the seven miles to State 154 and Old Saybrook.

Old Saybrook

Main Street (State 154) of Old Saybrook is a wide boulevard of low-level shops. A certain Olde Easyness exudes from the street, although it can turn crowded and busy quickly. Your best bet is to head straight on through if you're more inter-ested in the shore points than storefronts.

At the end of this wide boulevard, you'll see, on the left, the plain, white First Church of Christ, organized in "the Great Hall" of Saybrook Fort in 1646. In the early New World battle for power and geography, this area was first explored by the Dutch. But in 1632 the Earl of Warwick, head of the New England Council, granted a patent to fifteen men to settle and develop Saybrook, with the election of John Winthrop, Jr., as the first governor of the colony. (Those fifteen residents have proliferated to 9,500 today.) Winthrop had landed with the Pilgrims in Plymouth in 1620.

Originally, Saybrook encompassed 40,000 acres that today include the towns of Lyme, Chester, Westbrook, Essex, Old Saybrook, Old Lyme, Deep River, Clinton, and Killing-worth. The plan at the beginning was to establish a settlement "of quality" beyond the level of the Massachusetts Bay Colony. In 1635, twenty good and stout men from the Bay Colony were instructed to establish and hold claim to the Saybrook stronghold and develop it into a community of ele-vated values and achievements. In fact, the origin of the town name stems, some historians maintain, from Lord Say and

Sele and Lord Brooke of England. [Others trace the name to the combination of sea (Say) and Connecticut River (brook).]

Fort Saybrook was built, but the settlement of quality never materialized into the premier colony outpost first envisioned. Instead, over the early years Saybrook became a trading chip between Massachusetts and the new Connecticut Colony. When in the end Connecticut lost Springfield to Massachusetts but won Saybrook, it gained an important and strategic guardian settlement to the entrance of the great river. In addition, Connecticut later gained the prosperity of shipbuilding and the commercial harbors that developed in and around Saybrook.

During these early years several other important and curious historic events took place in Saybrook. One involved the increasingly autocratic ministers scattered around Connecticut towns and communities. To control these fractious enclaves and the exhausting religious and social battles among them, a convention of sixteen ministers and laymen met in September 1708 to draw up the Saybrook Platform designed to instill discipline in church government. The platform inaugurated a long period of peace among the sects by organizing a sort of association or union among the churches. The Saybrook Platform, issued by Thomas Short in New London, became the first publication printed in Connecticut.

Another historic curiosity is the establishment of the Collegiate Law School in Saybrook in 1701. The Puritan legislators granted a charter for "a Collegiate School wherein youth may be instructed in the arts and sciences, who through the blessing of Almighty God, may be fitted for publick imployments both in church and civill state." It was expensive to send students to Harvard, and besides, these founding ministers, all Harvard graduates, were disgruntled by the liberalism of Harvard. The trustees chose Saybrook as the site for the Collegiate School, but because of lack of funds the trustees voted to move the school to New Haven in 1716. After many shaky attempts to root itself in New Haven, the Collegiate School faced a desperate future until a wealthy trader with India came to the rescue with a substantial donation for financial support. The trustees had tempted the businessman with the prospect of eternal recognition by changing the name of the school in honor of the donor—Elihu Yale. Yale University, of course, went on to become one of the prestigious schools of the country.

When you reach the stop sign end of Main Street at Saybrook Point, you'll be turning right onto the State 154 shore points circle. But first you could turn left into the large parking lot in plain view, get out and walk along the pier by the Dock & Dine restaurant. Or turn into the parking lot of the Saybrook Point Inn and cruise by the adjoining marina with its chromy display of motor yachts.

Otherwise, ease down State 154 by the seashore. In short order you cross a long, narrow, low bridge across South Cove from Saybrook Point to Lynde Point. The bridge is a favorite for fishing hopefuls. The tower you see now and then ahead on the left is the Lynde Point Lighthouse.

Wind around through the now residential area, still on State 154, until seven-tenths of a mile later the shoreline appears. This long open section leads you past oceanfront homes on a choice stretch of shoreline overlooking Long Island Sound. No need to hurry past this soothing scene.

When you move away from the oceanfront about a mile later, look for a sign on the left to Castle Inn at Hartland Drive. The sign hangs a little before the stop sign. Turn left here and follow Hartland Drive past a few stop signs—practically one every block—to the Castle Inn on Cornfield Point. The fieldstone building evokes an early era of good living. In 1905 Mrs. George Watson Beach inherited 500 acres from a relative of Samuel Colt, the entrepreneur of Colt firearms. Completed two years later, the house was named Hartlands, and the Beach family lived at Hartlands for eighteen years. In 1925 the elaborate home was sold to a family that used the house during Prohibition as a base for rum-running. It was sold again and became the Philips Academy, a school for boys. Hartlands first became an inn—the Castle Inn—in the 1930s, and has been sold many times over the years. Today the Venetucci family is restoring the inn to its better days, as you'll see by the Victorian tenor of the lobby and the white-cloth dining room overlooking Long Island Sound.

When you return to State 154, turn left onto it and continue to the stop sign a very short distance away. Turn left and curve around to Indianapola Road (State 154), which curves right a little farther on. After passing a long salt marsh with tall, fuzzy-tipped grasses and wild pink roses on the right, the Old Saybrook Town Beach on the left appears in three-tenths of a mile. Here you can park, run your toes through the sand, and end the day with the tang of salt air as a trip memento.

In the Area

Camelot Cruises (East Haddam): 203-345-4507

Castle Inn (Old Saybrook): 203-388-4681

Dock & Dine restaurant (Saybrook Point): 203-388-4665

Gillette Castle State Park (Hadlyme): 203-526-2336

Goodspeed Opera House (East Haddam): 203-873-8668

Saybrook Point Inn (Old Saybrook): 203-395-2000; outside Connecticut: 1-800-243-0212; inside Connecticut: 1-800-733-0466

Thankful Arnold House (Haddam): 203-345-2400

RHODE ISLAND

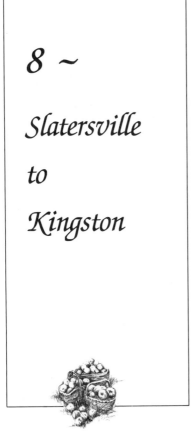

8 ~

Slatersville

to

Kingston

From Providence, Rhode Island: Take State 7 (Douglas Pike) north to State 5 north (Providence Pike) to State 102 in Slatersville. From Worcester, Massachusetts, take Massachusetts State 146 south to Massachusetts State 146A to Rhode Island State 102 beginning at Slatersville. This trip runs approximately fifty-four miles.

Highlights: Rhode Island's only covered bridge, Audubon Society woodland preserve, Arcadia recreation area, Tomaquag Indian Museum, roadside farmstands, homemade ice cream and candy shop, Great Swamp, University of Rhode Island main campus.

Slatersville to Parker Woodland

This trip cuts north to south through most of the western half of the state, giving you a taste of rural Rhode Island away from the coastal hubbub. Begin at the junctions of State 102 and State 5 crisscrossing in front of the Slatersville Plaza in Slatersville near the central northern state boundary. Head south on State 102 out of this small town on a comfortably wide two-lane highway for nearly two miles before the road narrows. A gravel and sand company shows up soon; keep on State 102 straight ahead into open country as you cross State 7, then two more miles later State 107.

By the time you reach the Gloucester township line 7.5 miles from Slatersville, you've eased through some tree-hugging sections of State 102. A small bridge crosses a broad-shouldered brook, and Sucker Pond shows its blue expanse by the side of the road. The sparsely populated country here hints at the early days. Excluding the Native Americans, Roger Williams has the recognition of establishing Rhode Island in 1636 after he was run out of Puritan Massachusetts. At Seekonk, now Providence, intrepid Williams founded the first colony in the New World with unfettered religious freedom.

Other individualistic religious colonies followed, including Anne Hutchinson's at Pocasset. Rhode Island freedom lured more headstrong followers of the tolerant, open life and in turn increased the collection of willful enclaves spreading up and down fish-rich Narragansett Bay. Whole groups of independent-minded people moved to new freedom-loving Rhode Island. In fact, the diverse seeds of this energetic individualism grew into such a tangled tradition that the cantankerous impulses that originally propelled them to seek wider freedom for all turned against them.

Small populations with stubborn, neighboring sub-groups can erupt into factions more boisterous than a country of strangers. When Roger Williams was appointed president of Rhode Island in 1654, the population scarcely totalled 1,500 stern and obstreperous colonists. Nevertheless, the colony grew steadily in commerce and characters. By the time of the Revolutionary War, the Rhode Island reputation for unbuttoned behavior had bloomed full strength. Rhode Island refused to send delegates to the 1787 Constitutional Convention in Philadelphia, and the following year rejected the U.S. Constitution by referendum. Two years later, after steamy debate and declarations, the Rhode Island delegates at their own convention held out to the stubborn last as the thirteenth state finally to ratify the U.S. Constitution, but only by a margin of two votes.

Typically, pugnacious Rhode Island had bolted into battling for the American Revolution for political and economic freedom, but once the battle faded into the past a year or two the state returned to its own path to the future. Centralized government, federated or not, held no quarter for a population that believed in the slogan, "United for war, separate for peace."

During all this political revolution Rhode Island revolutionized its economic front, too. Samuel Slater began the modern textile mills in the state and the nation. A skilled mechanic, he'd stolen out of England against a British law restricting emigration of the geniuses of the Industrial Revolution; he was part of the brain drain of the eighteenth century. From memory he constructed the first and most modern cotton-spinning machinery in the New World in 1790.

At Pawtucket ten years later Slater developed a hand-weave and mechanical loom combination in a large building for efficiency, but the inevitable resulted. The disgruntled, regimented weavers staged the first workers' strike in the United States. The machines won. By 1815 the power loom was invented, and unskilled women and children tended them. On the other hand, the burgeoning mills laid the foundation for early Rhode Island prosperity.

As you continue south on State 102, you'll cruise through Chepachet, a small, pleasant town with the white Chestnut Hill Antiques shop at a stop sign. Main Street with some oldish façades includes an 1809 shoe shop. Follow State 102 signs straight through town and into rural residential areas, crossing Rustic Hill Road, which clues you in to the countryside you're seeing.

The road narrows again as you cross first State 101 and then bigger US 6. About 1.5 miles after US 6, the road slants downhill from scattered hilltop homes for a soft view ahead. At the bottom of the hill, State 14 joins State 102 a short distance. The bridge over what appears to be a cozy pond on both sides actually extends into large, craggy Scituate Reservoir, mostly out of sight from the road.

Curve uphill three-quarters of a mile or so where an unusual fieldstone dam on the right catches the eye. Keep on following State 102 south as it curves to the right into Foster township (you'll see the sign).

Stay on State 102 south, about 4.5 miles later Biscuit Hill Road enters on the left, having gotten its name during the revolutionary years when a wagon loaded with biscuits for encamped French soldiers overturned. After crossing the Coventry town line, a half mile later on an open road a sign on the left announces the George C. Parker Woodland.

The original center-chimney Isaac Bowen house of 1765 stands a tenth of a mile from State 102 and the adjoining parking lot to the woodland trails. The eighty-three acres surrounding the yellow house were left to the Audubon Society as part of the 500-acre woodland in memory of William B. Spencer. The land ownership goes back to the 1642 Shawomet Purchase from the Narragansett Indians by colonists, through the Waterman family in 1672, Caleb Vaughn in 1760, and eventually to Eleanor Goff, who willed 200 acres to George Parker, who in 1938 offered and finally deeded some of the land to the Audubon Society, hence the name Parker Woodland.

The woodland nature center invites a get-out-of-your-car visit and a walk down the trails. A bird and animal watchers' site, the woodland offers relaxed and informative strolls among the trees. Now grown with maples, oaks, beech, and evergreens, in the early settling years the area supported small, hardscrabble farms and families. Cairns alongside the trails attest to this, although some people consider these piles of stones the work of precolonial Celtics or Narragansetts.

Arcadia and the Tomaquag Museum

From the Parker Woodland sign on State 102, continue south on State 102 through this backcountry. In about four miles you'll pass the West Greenwich township sign, and in another four miles proceed straight over I-95. State 3 and State 102 overlap a short distance; continue on State 3 (don't be tempted to turn left onto State 102). In about a mile turn right onto State 165 at a blinking yellow light. In three-tenths of a mile you'll pass under I-95. In 1.25 miles turn left at the first road after the interstate. A sign on a tree trunk says "Dovecrest Restaurant Trading Post Bed & Breakfast."

A mile and a half later down this deep, rural road suddenly appears the Arcadia Browning Mill Pond Recreation Area, which offers picnic tables, grassy slopes, pine trees, and a bathhouse for the pond beach swimmers. This pleasant place invites another stretch of the legs and rekindling of the spirit (if not a lunch for the stomach).

Continue another mile down this road and arrive at a T junction, with the Arcadia Warm Water Research Hatchery on the right corner. Turn right here and wind around two-tenths of a mile through a complex of homes to the Dovecrest Restaurant and Trading Post set uphill to the right. The menu includes some updated Native American foods; the trading post offers Indian goods to see and buy.

Across the street the Tomaquag Museum of the American Indian houses an intriguing collection of artifacts. Doors are open from March through November, Saturday and Sunday from noon to 3:00 P.M., or by appointment. This appealing museum comes in a small, weathered package on the outside, but inside the potent collection has intrigued and enlightened many children and their parents over the years.

Today more than 1,000 Narragansetts live in Rhode Island, as well as Mohegans, Pequots, Niantics, Cowesetts,

Nipmucs, and Wampanoags in neighboring southern New England areas. Artifacts in this museum reflect the tools and traditions of some of these local peoples. The person most remembered and associated with the museum is Princess Red Wing of Seven Crescents, who for many years showed visitors the museum. A legend in her area, Princess Red Wing at one time published a Narragansett newspaper, conducted educational tours, lectured across the country, and worked as a member of a research team for the United Nations from 1947 to 1970 before she became curator of the museum.

When Princess Red Wing was eighty-seven years old, she told this story during a private tour of her museum one day:

"Ages ago they had a thanksgiving every moon to thank the Great Spirit for something. We've merged into civilization, but we still have five thanksgivings. Your corn, your beans, your squash, your pumpkin, your melon, the Irish potato, the Hawaiian pineapple, the Italian tomato—all from the New World.

"Our first thanksgiving was for the giving of the sweet of the maple sap. Then our thanksgiving for the strawberry comes on the second Sunday in June. That's the nicest one of all because it's the thanksgiving of renewed friendships. Everybody makes up with everybody else, no matter how angry you are with your brother, your neighbor. Nobody gets into the strawberry dance with a grudge. Everybody is forgiven on that day and at peace. Because, you see, the strawberry is a peace offering.

"The third thanksgiving is celebrated for the giving of the green bean. When the people discovered they could eat the green bean as well as the white bean, they had to have another thanksgiving for the new dish. It comes on the third Sunday in July.

"The celebration for the giving of the cranberry is the fourth thanksgiving. The Great Spirit looked after his children of the forest because they lived so close to nature and nature's garden. He knew some weren't as fast as their brothers and sisters, some were slower. After the great frost, he turned the warm winds back so the people could get their harvest before winter, because they were slower, you see.

"Now he gave them a berry, but he had used all the sweetness in the raspberries, blackberries, and strawberries of summer. So they gathered in the tart cranberries just the same and made up their cranberry juice, cranberry sauce, Indian cranberry bread. And on the first Saturday in October we thank the Great Spirit for the cranberries.

"And now comes the thanksgiving you celebrate for the harvest and the garden, the fields and meadows. Many Pilgrims had died the previous harsh winter. Their crops were meager, their prospects dim. They faced another brutal winter and they were far from being in a grateful mood. Squanto stepped down to Plymouth. 'When things look dark, your crops are poor, many passing to the hereafter,' he said to Governor Bradford, 'that's the time for the biggest feast, the biggest thanks to your Creator to show him you're not complaining against your hard lot.'

"Governor Bradford answered, 'This would be good for my fainting people. Go call your people and tell them to come, and we will thank God together for what blessings we have.'

"The Indians came with their wild turkeys, their deer meat, their potatoes, their beans, their squash, their pumpkins—enough to feed all of Plymouth and themselves, and they cooked it up and ate and thanked God.

"In your schools they teach this was the first Thanksgiving. And to those Pilgrims it was. But to my ancestors, it was just another thanksgiving for the harvest of the garden, the forests, the fields, and meadows."

Great Swamp to the University of Rhode Island

When you return from the museum to the Arcadia Warm Water Research Hatchery, continue straight ahead with the double yellow line on what is called Old Nooseneck Hill Road. In about a mile you'll pass the Arcadia Management Area headquarters on the right, cross over a narrow bridge and onto a winding road in the trees and alongside a brook that feeds the fish hatchery. Another mile places you into more open farm fields where the next crossroad name spells out that you are indeed in backcountry—Skunk Hill Road.

In less than a half mile, turn left (the only way you can go) onto a connector to State 138 east and the small town of Wyoming. In about another half mile and when all this time you've been transported to the slow-down calm of the countryside, suddenly two surprises appear—the strip malls of Hope Valley and I-95. Head straight past the malls and straight under the interstate.

At exactly one mile from the interstate overpass, be sure to stop at the twenty-five-year-old Meadowbrook Herb Garden on the right, which is open all year. More than 250 varieties of organic and biodynamic herbs and plants grow in the greenhouse. The gift shop offers an appealing array of seasonings, books, crafts, and plants in addition to a wide selection of culinary and medicinal herbs, teas, and spices. In addition, owners Marjory and Tom Fortier schedule an extraordinary array of workshops on most weekends. Some of the lessons include Wheat Weaving, Herbs in the Classroom, Attracting Wildlife to Your Garden, Family Craft Day, Moss Day, and Pysanki Egg Decorating. The workshops are held in the flower-drying room out back past the greenhouses you won't be able to resist.

Continue east on State 138 past the Richard Elementary School at the junction of State 112. Three-quarters of a mile down this open road the shingled "Li'l Country Ice Cream" roadside stand might come in handy, especially in summer. Parking and tables make it easy. Fresh homemade chocolate candies add to the enticement.

Down the road a half mile you'll pass an egg farm, and then in another half mile State 138 narrows, giving you a half mile farther to watch for Heaton Orchard Road on the right (as State 138 curves left).

Turn right on Heaton Orchard Road and drive down the 1.5 miles to the T junction; the crossroad is State 2 (without a sign). Heaton Orchard Road takes you past a small plane airstrip and then large farm fields. Enjoy these fields because Rhode Island is suffering from the loss of farmland to housing and commercial development. Seventy-five percent of farmland in the state has been lost in the last half century. In 1930 dairy farms totaled 1,183 operations; 36 remain today. One family in this part of the state traces its roots back 300 years. To offset the demise of more farms to high modern costs and large commercial and tax assessments, a state program of buying development rights of a farm allows a family to retain the operation and keep the land for agricultural use. More than 2,500 acres of the 63,000 remaining agricultural acres have been saved this way.

Meanwhile, at the T junction, turn left and east on State 2. On the right you can pick your own strawberries at a roadside farm in June. One mile later a marker for the Great Swamp Fight stands on the right at an inauspicious entrance. The marker reads: "Three-quarters of a mile to the Southward on an island in the Great Swamp the Narragansett Indians were decisively defeated by the united forces of the Massachusetts Bay, Connecticut and Plymouth Colonies, Sunday December 19, 1675."

More lies behind the story on the marker than the carefully chosen words say. Drive the half mile to the circular parking area for the monument. Then walk the quarter mile on a wide, flat trail in the thick woods to the circle of stones around a rough-hewn obelisk. Four isolated boulders are chiseled with the names of the home colonies of the soldiers—Massachusetts, Connecticut, Rhode Island, Plymouth. A periphery trail leads a short distance farther into the solid land section of the swamp.

The causes and forces that led to the Great Swamp Fight of what is known as King Philip's War entertain many interpretations. Some say that the war resulted from a battle of culture against culture, not race against race. In many instances, Indian nations and tribes at that time had joined the Puritans in fighting against ancient Indian enemies. Some others say that the execution of three Indians sparked the war. Others suggest that Indian territory posed the main focus for the white land-grabbers, and that land was the seed cause of the conflict. Roger Williams himself declared that "God Land will be (as it is now) as great a God with us English as God Gold was with the Spaniards."

To be sure, prior to 1675 Rhode Island was by far and away largely Indian land, occupied by peoples who did not deed land as a sign of ownership. The outskirts of Providence remained raw frontier into which bounty hunters had only to travel a holler away to hunt wolves and wildcats. Encroaching commerce-minded, property-worshiping whites had eroded the original harmonious relations between Indians and Puritans. Relations had soured so much that Indians inevitably would lose nearly all cases in the white man's courts. Chief Metacomet of the Wampanoags especially grew increasingly agitated. Known as King Philip, son of Ousamequin, Metacomet said that land tract after land tract went to the white man by court ruling, "but a small part of the dominions of my ancestors remains. I am determined not to live till I have no country."

Metacomet had attempted for years before 1675 to build an alliance of regional peoples; some joined but more remained either neutral or allied with the Puritans. The pressure built until first blood was spilled in a battle in June 1675 as a result of heavy pressure from Massachusetts Puritans to usurp Indian land. When 1,100 Massachusetts, Connecticut, and Plymouth Colony soldiers, plus a few dozen Rhode Islanders, surprised Metacomet's forces in the Great Swamp December 19, 1675, a treasonous spy led to the near complete defeat of the Indian encampment. A fire spread through the wigwams, killing women, children, and warriors.

Then on March 26, 1676, Indian leaders Metacomet and Canonchet inflicted revenge by wiping out fifty-five Plymouth soldiers near Central Falls, Rhode Island. The next day they went six miles south to Providence, where Canonchet spared Roger Williams and his holdouts because of Williams's past support of Indians. Then Canonchet burned Providence. The following month the Indian leader was captured by Connecticut soldiers and executed. Metacomet was killed by a Wampanoag turncoat traitor in August 1676, which ended King Philip's War.

After returning to State 2 and the Great Swamp Fight marker on the highway, turn right and drive for one-tenth of a mile before turning right again at Liberty Lane. This takes you about two miles through a narrow, treed section and then past light industry to the stop sign at Kingstown Road. Turn right and go over the Amtrak railroad bridge. You're on State 138 again, this time in West Kingston and heading for Kingston. An entrance to the lower campus of the University of Rhode Island comes first on the left, but continue three-quarters of a mile farther to the main entrance at the hilltop with the stoplight. You are now on Upper College Road.

Davis Hall at the URI campus in Kingston

Two-tenths of a mile after turning left here, the campus entrance road leads you to the university information center on the right. Here schedules of events, lectures, talks, exhibits, and maps are available, plus campus newspapers and flyers. Farther along Upper College Road for a block on the left, you'll see the large quadrangle, with elaborate, granite-stone, turreted Davis Hall down the slope on the west side.

Turning right at this cross street to the quad on Fortin Road, you'll see the retail area of small shops and quick restaurants. Farther straight along Upper College Road are located the painting and photography galleries near the Fine Arts Center, which is across the street from the horticulture gardens.

Back on State 138 east, Kingston lies over the hill a short way and offers an attractive setting and a good place to end the trip.

In the Area

Arcadia Management Area (Exeter): 401-539-2356

Dovecrest Restaurant and Trading Post (Exeter): 401-539-7795

Meadowbrook Herb Garden (Wyoming): 401-539-7603

Parker Woodland (Coventry): 401-397-4474

Tomaquag Museum of the American Indian (Exeter): 401-322-8014; 401-539-2094; 401-539-7795

University of Rhode Island (Kingston): 401-792-7115

9 ~

Narragansett to Weekapaug

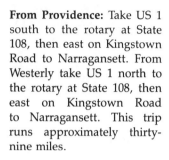

From Providence: Take US 1 south to the rotary at State 108, then east on Kingstown Road to Narragansett. From Westerly take US 1 north to the rotary at State 108, then east on Kingstown Road to Narragansett. This trip runs approximately thirty-nine miles.

Highlights: The Towers, many state beaches, Point Judith Coast Guard Lighthouse, Block Island views, Fort Ninigret Memorial, many inlets and coves.

Narragansett to Point Judith

The southernmost coastline of Rhode Island is a low-keyed, relatively undeveloped area with a ragged shoreline and many roads leading to the deep blue waters of Block Island Sound. The area husbands extensive woodlands on its picturesque, rocky-edged peninsulas, backwater salt marshes, inlets, harbors, coves, ponds, and ports. This trip explores some of these easygoing sites.

In summer the Rhode Island coastline of the great Atlantic becomes a favorite for swimmers and loungers, especially at the many state beaches, although many private beaches compete for the sun and sand. Narragansett Town Beach is one of these prized (public) areas for swimming, sunning, and surfing. It curves like a wide C at the end of a constant sweep of waves onto good sand and is a focal point of the town.

The new Village Inn complex behind the beach makes an updated sight too, and is across the way from our starting point—the Towers, the most well-known and obvious landmark of Narragansett. The turreted, round-stone building on the shoreline remains the last of the Narragansett Pier Casino that Stanford White, the famous architect in the last of the nineteenth century, built as part of the summer social scene that made the seacoast town famous. (Stanford White achieved other fame by being shot by the husband of Evelyn Nesbit Thaw in Madison Square Garden for having an affair with his fame-loving wife.)

The local chamber of commerce in the ground-level office of the turret next to the shoreline distributes information and brochures about the area; you can park your car directly in front of the office or in an adjoining lot that overlooks the town beach to the left, the Atlantic to the right.

Begin by heading south on US 1A, which passes under the Towers. One of the delights of much of this trip is that you can see the ocean from paralleling roads; no high walls block the eyeline, as you'll notice right away for the first half mile or so. Then the road moves past a stone "kiosk" in the two-lane highway and sends you inland slightly. Be sure to stay on US 1A south.

Along here the road winds past stone cottages and somewhat elaborate shoreside homes. About a quarter mile past the private Point Judith Country Club, a large stone turret entrance announces a driveway, which is almost emblematic of the grander homes in the area. If Rhode Island needed another description, the "Turret State" would be a good one. Keep an eye out too throughout the trip for the many varieties of stone walls, some loosely piled, some smooth-surfaced, high, low—but usually long. Good use of stone taken from cleared fields shows up in some fine-looking stone houses as well, their message clearly stating a certain sturdy and unshakeable presence of the history and tradition that contributed to building them. Two-tenths of a mile later on the right a beautifully constructed wall enclosing a secondary school operated by the Christian Brothers is another example of how stone can cultivate a different feeling, as it does here lining a long, wide, clipped field.

About a half mile later, with wild grapes and beach plums growing alongside the road, the shoreline reappears. Before long the Scarborough State Beach complex comes into view, its striking smooth stone bathhouse and cabanas catching the eye for their clean lines and modern tone. This is one of the more attractive beaches to visit and is known for its exuberant body surfing on the endless roll of long-breaking waves.

A mile and a half later comes a stop sign. Continue straight ahead to Point Judith, as a sign instructs. A half mile later veer left, passing Camp Crown Fishing Area, and then shortly again approaching the Coast Guard station and lighthouse. The octagonal lighthouse was the second built here, in 1816, after the original wooden structure was blown apart by what is known as the Great Gale of September 1815. This important, strategic point of land became an early warning location as far back as the American Revolution, when a beacon tower was built.

Follow the quick U-bend of the road and immediately to the right steer up a short, steep driveway to an abandoned motel. This takes you to a high-perched parking area overlooking the lighthouse and Coast Guard station. Four benches are positioned wide apart along a grassy cliff. Somewhere two

The lighthouse at Point Judith looks toward Block Island

miles off the lighthouse the last German U-boat submarine was sunk during World War II.

This indeed is a point of land, almost a stiletto. The view wraps around an invigorating sweep of ocean. Most likely fishing boats will be prowling the deep for tuna, marlin, and lobsters. The seemingly three-section chunk of Block Island breaks the horizon slightly to the right. To the left the Rhode Island coastline stretches northward. This is a place to linger and inhale the ocean air. Enjoy! Enjoy!

Galilee to Green Hill Beach

After returning to the stop sign at State 108, turn left onto State 108. Then a quarter mile later turn left on Sand Hill Cove Road with the sign directing you this way toward Captain Wheeler Memorial Beach. The next mile and a half to Galilee takes you on a pleasant drive past sand dunes and beach houses, wild beach roses and gray-shingled cottages.

All of a sudden you approach the State Pier complex with a passenger and auto ferry to Block Island. The blinking yellow light and curve in the road guide you around the back of the Dutch Inn. As you loop around the inn, a stop sign lets you see the ferry trip–related shops and parking lots to the left. To the right you'll notice the warehouses and piers of the working fishing fleet coming and going from Galilee. This is the port of Galilee, located on Point Judith; the ferry trip is known as the Point Judith Island Ferry Dock.

The trip to Block Island, nine miles to sea, has become a popular summer excursion. The island has an intriguing history, beginning geologically with moraines formed from glacial debris as the last Ice Age receded. The island rises 204 feet at its highest elevation and sports more than 360 spring-fed freshwater ponds, some of them 60 feet deep. The 100-acre Great Salt Pond, the only salt pond on the island, nearly divides the isle in half.

Evidently, Native Americans lived on the island for generations before whites arrived. The answer to which Europeans discovered the island is up for speculation. Some say that the Vikings set their wandering feet ashore. The Italian navigator Verrazano definitely sailed along its coast in 1524, since his journals record that he compared the island to the Island of Rhodes, hence, the name of the state. Apparently, he didn't land, or if he did (who could resist?), he made no note of it.

On the other hand, Captain Adrien Block, the Dutch explorer, did for sure and true set foot on the island, disembarking from his ship, the *Restless*, in 1614. In his journal he records how well the Indians welcomed and received him, presenting his crew with succotash, clams, hominy, fish, and game. Although Captain Block and other Dutch never settled on the island, he named it Adriaen's Eyland. Not until 1661 did the first whites make a formal survey of the land and set up house. Three years later the island was admitted to the Rhode Island Colony and incorporated as New Shoreham in 1672.

A hardscrabble but peaceful life ensued until seventeen years later, when certain profiteering French sailors, disguised as friendly English, duped and overwhelmed the islanders, ransacking the settlement and its people. For scores of years afterward, Block Island suffered many intrusions and piracies. During the American Revolution, for instance, deserters and outlaws escaped to the isolated, little-known island. But the islanders got their revenge, best served, of course, on a cold plate. Whenever they noticed the riffraff leaving the island to surprise and rob the mainlanders, the islanders ignited their ready barrels of tar as smoky warnings to be seen across the waters that the no-goods were trying to sneak into the mainland villages and have their way. The warned and hard-eyed mainlanders then got rid of the criminals for the islanders.

Meanwhile, decades passed with the gradual development of small farms to support the secluded population. Such seclusion was appealing to Captain Kidd as well; stories persist that he buried some of his piratical treasures on the island, and the search for them continues. But along with farming, fishing too was a major life support system, as it is with most similar islands. So deeply seeded and rooted was fishing that entrance into manhood was measured according to a boy's first fishing trip, not his years.

Another noted and perhaps too neglected fact is that Sarah Sands, throughout the early turbulent years that formed the country, served the island as surgeon and physician and is therefore said to be the first woman doctor in the English colonies.

Finally, in 1880 the federal government laid a telegraph cable from Block Island to Point Judith and opened up the island to the faster and faster pace of the modern world.

If you wish to avoid the left turn at the stop sign north of the Dutch Inn and the ferry area too, turn right. The fishing fleet works directly across the way now; the processing plants and piers for the large fishing boats are plainly in sight. A breach separates Galilee and Jerusalem on the close but unconnected shore straight across the entrance channel to Point Judith Pond. So you have to return on the point to proceed southward on the coastline. This means that after turning right at the Dutch Inn, you drive a short distance to Galilee Road and turn right again here. In less than five minutes of wide-open, pleasant driving you'll come to State 108. Turn left on State 108 north and drive nearly five miles through a half dozen signal lights to the junction of US 1; turn left for US 1 south.

Many sections of US 1, the first and famous federal highway that follows the Eastern Seaboard, have a smudged reputation for congested driving, with lots of shops lining the roadside. This section offers nothing of the sort. For the next dozen miles or so, US 1 is instead very pleasant, easy cruising through forested land on a well-controlled double highway.

Along this stretch some turnoffs might interest you. About 4.5 miles from where you got on US 1, turn down a good access road to Jerusalem, the town directly across from Galilee and the Block Island Ferry Dock. A half mile farther the summer-operating Theatre by the Sea might have a performance that fits into your schedule. As you pass the Charlestown town line sign about four miles later, another mile leads you to the road for the Royal Indian Burial Ground on the right a short way off the main road. Here Narragansett sachems (chiefs) are buried.

After a couple more miles, look for a left-turn sign to the Charlestown Chamber of Commerce Tourist Information Center. This is a good place to find answers to questions about the area and get an enlarged, detailed map of Charlestown with all its side roads and coves and plenty of suggestions on what to see in the area. Actually, the local map contains a much more accurate depiction of the region than the state map, which shows some discrepancies.

Before moving on down US 1, take a side trip to Fort Ninigret for a wonderful spot to snack or lunch. It lies at the end of a snub-nosed cove lined with woodlands against blue waters, with maybe a small sailboat or two moving through the inlet. To get there from the Tourist Information Center, turn left going outside the parking lot of the center (this road is US 1A) for 1.3 miles to US 1. Drive onto US 1 for—yes—one-tenth of a mile. So keep to the right and prepare to turn off right away, onto Old Post Road. The fort is two-tenths of a mile farther. At one time the fort was considered to be prehistoric mounds, but it's now thought to be the site of a Dutch trading post. At the entrance to the access road, a marker on an upright stone reads: "South of this spot is located Fort Ninigret marked by the State of Rhode Island as a memorial of the Narragansett and Niantic Indians the unwavering friends and allies of our fathers."

A tenth of a mile down the access road takes you to the memorial, which is simple in design but irresistible for its setting. A large boulder, inscribed similarly to the one at the fort, in the center of a wide, encircling pipe fence signifies the spot. This restful place invites a stroll and some time to linger a while as you take in the rich seacoast colors of ocean blue against woodland green.

Returning on the access road, turn right and continue on Old Post Road for a half mile where a Charlestown center of church, art gallery, public library, and country village cemetery brings you back to what you might have thought was gone entirely—town life. In another half mile or so, veer right at a Y junction with a fire station on the right. This leads to the Charlestown Beach, the road to which comes up soon after Niantic Drive and Atlantic Drive. Another small business complex—a deli, fish market, ice cream shop—marks where you turn right onto Charlestown Beach Road. Follow the yellow line all the way down this road.

At the shore either park in the lot or continue driving a short distance past the lot, turn right, and cruise down to the end of a sand-gravel road that takes you past beachfront summer cottages on stilts, sand dunes, and wild beach roses. This road paralleling the beach ends in eight-tenths of a mile at the Charlestown Beachway Camping Area, where a dune restoration project of planting drift-resistant grasses is in progress.

Weekapaug

To proceed southward on the coast, return by way of the same Charlestown Beach Road to US 1. Throughout this trip and as you drive south now toward Westerly, many Indian names identify the ponds, inlets, forests, roads, and towns—Ninigret Pond and National Wildlife Refuge, Watchaug Pond, Quonochontaug fishing area, the town of Matunuck, Niantic Highway. Some of the names are tongue-trippers, some bewilderingly long, but all of them show a colorful and lasting influence of the native tribes on Rhode Island. Throughout the state many of the town and city names that have become familiar derive from original Indian words and phrases. The city of Woonsocket inherited its name from Miswosakit, which means "at the very steep hill." (Woonsocket Hill is located in North Smithfield.) *Pawtucket* means "waterfall place." *Apponaug* means "shellfish," and *Sakonnet* is redesigned from the Indian phrase meaning "that haunt of the wild goose." Conanicut Island is named for the Narragansett sachem leader Canonicus. The list of how the Nipmucks, Pequots, Narragansetts, Nantics, Wampanoags, and other tribes stamped their signatures on the state is extensive.

After you pass the Westerly town line, keep on the lookout for US 1A about a mile later. Turn left toward Weekapaug (another Indian reference) and about 1.5 miles later turn left onto Weekapaug Road. The next half mile leads you past a charming inlet, probably with white herons standing highnecked and long-legged in the muck. The road passes along a small marina and houses with white fences and pink and red roses growing in and out of the pickets.

At the low cement bridge go straight and ease past the old Victorian gray-shingled cottages that line the shoreline. A half mile later at the stop sign, turn right, then left right away, and soon you'll come to a relatively elevated ledge where you can park directly overlooking the coastline. This offers a relaxing spot with refreshing views of Block Island straight out to sea, the rocky shoreline with gentle waves cresting white against the sand-colored boulders, and old-time cottages doing the same thing you are, only longer.

This is a good place to end the trip, but if curiosity gets the better of you, follow this road as it veers to the left and right, but in three-tenths of a mile it dead-ends at a private beach entrance. Simply turn around and return to the cement bridge at the second stop sign, turn left onto Atlantic Road and the bridge, and drive past the private beach club on the left, fish restaurants and clam shacks on the right. The road takes you past Winnapaug Pond on the right, a tidal marsh of water birds and tall grasses. Then drive 1.5 miles from the bridge to the Westerly Town Beach where you'll find an amusement park with its attendant tourist shops and the Misquamicut State Beach, too. A right turn and another mile make the second end of this trip at US 1A.

In the Area

Block Island Ferry, all reservations: 401-783-4613

Charlestown Chamber of Commerce Tourist Information Center (Charlestown): 401-364-3878

The Dutch Inn, Port of Galilee (Narragansett): 401-789-9341, -9342, -9343, -9344

Narragansett Chamber of Commerce Visitors Center (Narragansett): 401-783-7121

Point Judith Lighthouse (Narragansett): 401-789-0444

The Village Inn (Narragansett): 1-800-843-7437

10 ~

Narragansett to Newport

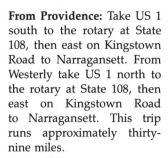

From Providence: Take US 1 south to the rotary at State 108, then east on Kingstown Road to Narragansett. From Westerly take US 1 north to the rotary at State 108, then east on Kingstown Road to Narragansett. This trip runs approximately thirty-nine miles.

Highlights: The Towers, Silas Casey Farm, Gilbert Stuart birthplace, South Ferry Church, University of Rhode Island Narragansett Bay campus, Jamestown Bridge, Conanicut Island, Newport Bridge, Newport mansions, Brenton Point State Park.

Narragansett to Saunderstown

Although this is a short trip overall, it covers an impressive range of scenes. The trip begins at a town beach, passes along a modest residential section, crosses twice the splendid Narragansett Bay, follows the tree-tight edge of Conanicut Island, visits the splendor of the Newport mansions, and ends with the elemental simplicity of the seashore.

Begin as you did trip number nine (Chapter 9)—at the Towers in Narragansett. Built by the renowned (and infamous)

Stanford White as a centerpoint of the casino summer social life around the turn of the century for this popular town, the Towers is a seaside stone-and-turreted building straddling US 1A. The local chamber of commerce in the bottom level of the tower by the shore distributes brochures and information about the immediate area.

From the Towers drive north along US 1A as it follows the curves of Narragansett Town Beach, a popular summer spot for its half-moon sandy expanse at the end of a funnellike harbor. The Village Inn, a clean-line, modern complex, overlooks the beach to your left as you drive past the gray-colored hotel toward the town bathhouse and cabanas. In seven-tenths of a mile the highway veers away from the shore into a residential area. Broad-shouldered maples, sidewalks, and wide road shoulders make it attractive to bicyclists, which in summer you'll likely see on their way to the flat shoreline along the town beach and south of the Towers.

The road rises slightly and gradually to higher land as you cross a small bridge over a narrow ocean inlet. This is cruise-along country by stone-wall estates with stone turrets here and there announcing their driveway entrances and rose-covered walls decorating the property fronts. About three miles north of the Towers, an unusual border of maple trees lines the road, making the drive feel like you are entering a tunnel of trees, which continues for about a half mile.

Glimpses of the great bay break the woodlands on the right here now and then as you proceed north on US 1A, also called Boston Neck Road.

A mile and a half from the end of the maple tree alley, turn right at the signal light onto South Ferry Road for three interesting stops in a relatively short distance on this dead-end road. The first attraction in three-quarters of a mile needs no words to point it out. It suddenly appears on the left after a sharp rise of the road—South Ferry Church. This hilltop, isolated, charmer of a church stands small and narrow, evoking the simple yesteryears, its almost scalloplike shingle façade standing out for its rare design. A one-car parking slot in front of the church lets you take a longer look than you can speeding by, which you probably wouldn't be able to do anyway. The church was established in 1851 originally as the Narragansett Baptist Church, which used to be visible as a landmark on this once-cleared hilltop for miles in every direction. It's now on the National Register of Historic Places.

Shortly over the hill turn right into the University of Rhode Island Narragansett Bay campus where the Graduate School of Oceanography and environmental research studies are conducted. The school has a relatively small campus, circling halfway around the main buildings where, on your right, a sign by the road directs you to the Visitors' Center. A few aquarium displays, some sea-life artifacts, and a video presentation are open to the public.

For the third stop, return to the South Ferry Road and turn right from the campus entrance. Continue down a steep slant of the road a short distance to the shoreline. This road's end provides access for researchers and their boats to the bay as well as for the public to go fishing and for you to stop and enjoy the view. To the left arches the Jamestown Bridge, which you'll be crossing fairly soon, as well as water-level views of the wide-open Narragansett Bay half encircling you.

When you return to US 1A, turn right and north at the signal light and continue through wooded areas. From South Ferry Road, 1.6 miles later on the left the rather unobtrusive Casey Farm comes into view. This 1750 farm is open to tours, if your schedule coincides, but if not you can see the old stone barn and the corrals of stone walls and feel the ancient ambience of the place. The farm is protected and maintained by the Society for the Preservation of New England Antiquities.

Three-quarters of a mile farther north on US 1A is the turnoff to the left for the birthplace of Gilbert Stuart. The marker at the side of the road reads: "A mile westward stands the snuff mill where was born December 3, 1755, America's foremost portrait painter—the Wedgewood House."

In a barnlike house, Stuart was born of a Scot who operated America's first snuff-grinder in 1755. In school at Newport the young boy's drawings and paintings of dogs and copies of other pictures evidently served ample notice to teachers that his talent was unusual indeed. He graduated to painting portraits of prominent Newport residents at an early age. Then to develop his skills and following the tradition of the formative years of the emerging new nation, he went to the Old World, where the arts were more rooted and teachers and colleagues more seasoned and numerous.

After two years in Scotland, Stuart returned to America until the outbreak of the Revolutionary War. For the future fame and legacy he was to bestow on the United States, his sympathies for the Tory side of the Revolution evidently mattered not at all in the long run. Art won out. When the war ignited, he left America again and lived and worked in England. By 1788 his services were in such demand that he opened his own studio, after apprenticing with famed artist Benjamin West. He then moved to Ireland, but this led to a series of burdensome debts, and in 1792 he returned to America to regain his balance.

This was when he began his portraits of George Washington—at least 124 of them. He lived in Boston a while, where the famous unfinished Athenaeum Head, which is seen every day on the U.S. one-dollar bill, was commissioned by Martha Washington. In Newport, where Stuart also lived later in life, he was commissioned in 1800 by the General Assembly of Rhode Island to paint portraits of Washington; he was paid $1,200 by the state, $200 for the frame. The pictures were hung in the Senate chambers of the state houses in Newport and Providence. Stuart's elegant portrait style was modeled on the works of his English mentors, Reynolds and Gainsborough. Stuart died in 1828, leaving nearly 1,000 portraits.

Conanicut Island

Less than a mile from Snuff Mill Road, which leads to Gilbert Stuart's birthplace, follow the signs to State 138 east over the Jamestown Bridge to Conanicut Island. The ride over the new bridge is spectacular. (The old bridge on the right is used now for fishing.) Riding high and wide, you can see Narragansett Bay and its long stretch on both sides of you—the lilliputian islands, the flat blues of the bay, the Atlantic far to the right. The 1.5-mile bridge trip puts Narragansett Bay into grand perspective and gives you a sea gull's view of this mesmerizing corner of the world.

Continue one mile on State 138 straight ahead, moving to the left lane as you approach a stop sign (most of the other traffic veers to the right). At the stop sign, turn left. Here begins East Shore Road, which takes you on a tight country drive. You will feel as if you were far beyond the congested network of the doings in the big city of Newport, which is coming up as the next part of the trip.

Conanicut Island was named after the sachem (chief) Canonicus of the Narragansetts when Roger Williams arrived in what is now known as Rhode Island. The island is about nine miles long. English Quakers formed the largest group of early settlers, later followed by Portuguese. The land was more cleared than it is today. Agricultural and dairy farms were relatively plentiful, as was the raising of sheep, which were exported through Newport.

Before the bridges were constructed, ferries transported passengers and vehicles to the island from either Saunderstown or Newport. Three score years ago the cost was ninety cents a vehicle, fifteen cents a passenger. Cost today to go over the Newport bridge: $2.00 a vehicle, each way. If

119

knowing this history makes you feel better about paying the toll as you drive over State 138 bisecting Conanicut Island, remember too that George Washington traveled the same way in March 1781 on his way to Newport to confer with Rochambeau about plans to defeat Cornwallis at Yorktown, Virginia.

Today this island is the land of small cottages in the woods, and it is enjoyable for this alone. Cruise along here, take your time, take pleasure in small surprises. About a mile on the way, the road slants down to shore level with quick sights of the water through scrub brush. The land slopes to water's edge, and the breezes from the great bay are pleasant and fragrant.

The deeply wooded area continues along this straight and narrow road with virtually no shoulder. So the driving is perforce slow paced.

Unfortunately, the end point of Conanicut Island is locked away from public enjoyment by private owners and houses. However, if you do want to sneak a peek at the bay, here's how to do it:

At the end of the East Shore Road with its double yellow line (at a little more than three miles), turn right onto an unmarked road, resisting the tendency to turn left. In one-tenth of a mile the bay comes into view as you veer to the right again onto a bumpy dirt road. This rather hidden road parallels the shoreline and is open and airy so you can see the bay far and wide. The road curves in an oblong for a quarter mile back to East Shore Road. Once you're at this point, you'll recognize that, in fact, you've already driven past this asphalt point.

So turn right and retrace the short distance on East Shore Road again to the stop sign. This time turn left, and a quarter mile later you'll reach a stop sign at North Main Road. Turn right and proceed back down the middle of Conanicut Island. It's another straight-and-narrow road with no shoulder, and it's densely wooded on both sides.

When 2.5 miles later you pass a lake on your left, you're a quarter mile away from the signal light at State 138. You'll recognize that you've made a full circle to a point just off the Jamestown Bridge. Therefore, turn left at the light onto State 138 and drive the half mile east to the stop sign at East Shore Road where you began the circle, only this time stay to the right with most of the traffic, which follows State 138 toward Newport.

Newport

One mile after turning right on State 138 toward the Newport Bridge, pay your toll and drive onto another spectacular high-suspension view of Narragansett Bay. As you curve up and over the waters, the bay reveals its aesthetic length on both sides. Rose Island is close by on the right, and in summer most likely sailboats of all sizes and colors will be tilting their graceful way to and fro below.

After nearly three miles of driving across the sky, steer down to earth again and turn right onto the downtown Newport exit, passing a marina and keeping on State 138 south straight into the heart of town. You pass through the center of Braman's Cemetery, with Jewish gravestones on the right, Christian on the left.

A half mile later the route takes you directly to the Visitors' Information Center operated by the Newport Country Convention and Visitors Bureau at the transportation terminal on the right. If you want brochures and tickets to some tours, park inside the garage and get your ticket validated for a half hour of free parking. Otherwise, continue on America's Cup Avenue (the same road that brought you to this point). It takes you through the heart of town a short distance past an elegant marina with sleek yachts plainly visible. Keep to the right because in a little more than a quarter mile you'll turn left onto Memorial Boulevard. The landmark for this turn is the Newport Bay Club building made of finished stone walls directly facing you broadside. Continue on Memorial Boulevard past Spring Street, then at the next block turn right onto Bellevue Avenue, the street of the mansions.

Newport today is a well-trimmed magnet for summer folk and fun. The actual city of Newport proper and its relevant environs are shaped somewhat like Italy with a high shoe top, heel, and a big front foot, although overall it's connected to the island of Rhode Island (previously known as Aquidneck), the largest in Narragansett Bay. The town name is likely taken from the Newport of the Isle of Wight. Founded in 1639, the New World Newport contained important historical leverages during the formation of the United States as a growing political and economic power, not to mention the geographical location of Newport as an extraordinary setting for mercantile harbors and, later, as a playground for high society.

Shipbuilding became a prosperous industry early on, sending commerce from the town to the Caribbean and other nearby areas. At the same time, Newport drew in people of dissent, especially Quakers who left England for the sake of religious safety and tolerance. In 1672, for instance, two prominent leaders of religious freedom—George Fox, a Quaker, and Roger Williams—debated in Newport. Rhode Island was known as a trademark of freedom, and this too drew Ben Franklin's brother James from Boston to print pamphlets and eventually, in 1732, to found the *Rhode Island Gazette,* the first newspaper in the state.

Thirty years later Newport had nearly 900 houses and half this in warehouses and stores. Its farming, fishing, and shipbuilding were turning the port town into a wealthy commercial and financial center on the Eastern Seaboard. But all was not freedom as advertised, because the African slave trade ranked high as a Rhode Island "industry" that created fortunes for slave traders and their estimated sixty ships engaged in human traffic.

Newport also had about fifty ships under privateers, the private shipowners and captains licensed by the state to attack and destroy enemy commercial ships. Some of these privateers, such as the notorious Captain Kidd, who anchored and visited friends in the great bay, turned to piracy and smudged Newport's reputation further.

The first clear sign of the high social life here occurred in the mid-1700s when Southern families brought their aristocratic ways and entourages to town for the cool summer months. Then came the English colonists from the West Indies. Newport was headed, some thought, to be the splendid center of the New World for its financial, cultural, intellectual, and social elite. But the revolution interrupted the continuum, and Newport suffered from the damage and debilitation of the complicated war among the British, the French, and some of the vacillating Indian nations.

Well into the nineteenth century, Newport recovered its commercial and social stability. About this time the Irish added another wave of immigrants to the cultural mix, and long-term traditions vied for dominance. One of them, however, was shared by all involved—Newport punch, a compound of rum, lime juice, arrack, and loaf sugar (sugar cubes).

By 1830 Newport revived its checkered reputation as a summer resort area for people mostly from the South and Cuba. A couple of rather expensive homes were built on Bellevue Avenue, but not much else of note. The next few decades sailed on an even keel until after the Civil War, when Newport once again jumped with an exuberant summer scene. In came national tennis championships, roller skating, telephones, and automobiles toward the end of the century—and the "gilded years" of 1890 to 1914.

The wealthy, the rich, and what would today be called the ultrarich grabbed the choice cliffs and beaches to build elaborate show palaces reminiscent of the castles of European royalty. The rich, who controlled profits without an income tax to distribute the wealth back to the people who provided their wealth in the first place, barricaded themselves socially. If intruders to their beaches, for instance, crossed the socially sanctimonious lines, hired scouts rushed to intercept them, demanding their names, and, if not recognized, forcing them off the captured beaches and back to what they called the "common beaches." Members of this high society often referred to the townspeople as "our footstools."

Part of the high social scene was extravagant parties costing $300,000 a season for one household, some single parties and balls costing $100,000. But the "footstools" retaliated by charging outlandish prices for their goods and services, thereby earning enough money to take them through the rest of the year when the "cottagers" left after their eleven-week splurge.

Mrs. William Astor wore the social crown of the Bellevue group, and when the time arrived for her pinnacle event, only 400 (because that's what her ballroom held) of the Social Register were invited. Reputations could be besmirched if certain climbers were snubbed. Henry Lehr's "Dogs' Dinners" of stewed liver, fricassee of bone, and shredded dog biscuit for 100 canine guests were among the novelties of the elite. "Hen dinners," in which only women were invited, were popular too for a time.

The Gilded Age died with World War I. No longer did ninety guests attend the indulgent banquets, parties, and balls. What remains of the era are the mansions, which in the "cutesiness" of the upper crust of the social pie were called "cottages." The Preservation Society of Newport County operates tours for many of these elaborate estates. Tickets are sold at the mansions themselves; the cost is prorated according to how many you wish to visit.

As you drive down Bellevue Avenue many more mansions of lesser repute but equally elaborate style line the celebrated street. Some of the more well-known mansions include the Elms, Château-sur-Mer, Rosecliff, and Marble House. But the Breakers is the one recognized as the most ornamental example of the pretentious set. The original house, owned by Cornelius Vanderbilt, burned in 1893. (He made his fortune in railroads and steamships.) To avoid another fire, Vanderbilt and his designer Richard Morris Hunt used no wood for the structure, only brick, stone, and steel. Even the original heating system for the kitchen was built underground sufficiently away from the house itself.

The Breakers was built in two years by hundreds of workers on the eleven-acre estate grounds at the edge of the Atlantic at Ochre Point. It was named for the color of the waves that broke against the rocky shore. The interior is embellished and overlaid with fine detail and carvings with gold leaf. Pillars and floors and walls are made of fine marble, some of it light green cipollino marble. Thirty-three of the seventy rooms were given over to the staff of forty, half of which worked inside, the other half outside. (Vanderbilt's New York residence, which he used during the rest of the year, had 100 rooms and staff enough to mount a dinner for 200 people at any declared time.)

A display of richness at the Breakers was designed to awe visitors and, in the four summers Vanderbilt lived there, business consultants and wheeler-dealers. The two-story dining room alone looks like one of the most lavish European castle ballrooms. Everywhere are oriental rugs of high quality and imperial length, tapestries to impress, furnishings to gape at, chandeliers and painted ceilings to overwhelm. Exquisite marble pillars are rounded on one side, squared off on the other. Large, wooden library doors were designed and carved specifically for the mansion, and huge crews of skilled stonecutters chiseled fine detail on the interior walls everywhere. Individual rooms display separate opulent motifs and ambiences. Balustrades give off a sumptuous richness, and the balcony/hallway overlooking the Great Room (measuring fifty

The Breakers

feet wide and high in every direction) is decorated with busts of Bacchus, depicted with grapes entwined around his head as the Greek god of wine, revelry, orgy, and good times.

Down the avenue stands Marble House, another example well known for its extravagance. More than 500,000 cubic feet of marble were used in this spectacle. This too was built by a Vanderbilt—William—to give to his wife in 1888 as a summer cottage, also designed by Richard Morris Hunt. The house took four years and $11 million to build. Everywhere marble shines on the walls, floors, and ceiling. Gold leaf, crystal chandeliers, beveled glass doors, seventy-pound dining table chairs requiring footmen to move them for guests, and other garish displays fill the house.

Handsome, giant wrought-iron gates greet you at the entrance. Inside the front door, exquisite tapestries hang on either side, covering much of the marble wall from floor to high ceiling. A marble staircase to the left flows upward in a graceful, wide arc, while to the right the glow from the gold-leaf, gold-tone ballroom is seen through full-length glass doors. Scenes of adventure and raucous love from Greek mythology decorate the ballroom walls. Other rooms depict and display other period themes of wealth and artifacts. At the top of the staircase alcove rooms for men and women are decorated according to the roles of the sexes of the time. From a back upstairs room, you can view a tea house in a corner of the grounds at the edge of the ocean. In one of the front bedrooms, where rich fabric covers the walls, the bed is placed on a raised platform in keeping with the tradition of royalty of the Old World that kings and queens do not sleep on the same level as their subjects.

On and on the Bellevue Avenue display goes, with one mansion after another. Some of them remain in private hands, but most don't. They've turned into tourist attractions and museums of a bygone era. They have their attraction as a reference point in American history, and they do offer beautiful sights of workmanship, design, and estate grounds. It's interesting too to see up close how the downstairs kitchens, with the inevitable French chef, worked for the upstairs people, how the butler protected the wine cellar from pilfering, how in Marble House the female help in their quarters downstairs were separated from the male help in their quarters upstairs by an iron barrier gate.

Continue down Bellevue Avenue until you reach the end of the way where you must follow the curving road to the right. Drive easily onto what is now the eleven-mile Ocean View loop. Soon you open onto scenes of the ocean and rocky shoreline as you dip and rise slightly, curve in and out. You can continue following this road; signs direct you back to the Ruggles Avenue start of the mansion row on Bellevue Avenue.

On the other hand, the stone building set on a knoll to the right at Brenton Point State Park makes a good stopping point. Park your car in the lot facing the shore, walk across the road, climb down to the rocky coastline, and linger a while. If you're lucky, a tall ship or two will sail across the bay toward the Atlantic Ocean. Otherwise, look to the earthly beauty Rhode Island offers as one of the real treasures of the world.

In the Area

The Breakers (Newport): 401-847-1000

Brenton Point State Park (Newport): 401-847-2400

Château-sur-Mer (Newport): 401-847-1000

The Elms (Newport): 401-847-1000

Gilbert Stuart Birthplace (North Kingston): 401-294-3001

Marble House (Newport): 401-847-1000

Narragansett Chamber of Commerce Visitors' Center
(Narragansett): 401-783-7121

Newport Visitors' Bureau (Newport): 401-849-8098; 1-800-326-6030

Rosecliff (Newport): 401-847-1000

Casey Farm (Saunderstown): 401-227-3956

University of Rhode Island Narragansett Bay campus (Narragansett): 401-792-6211

The Village Inn (Narragansett): 1-800-843-7437

Index

Other titles in the Country Roads series:

Country Roads of Florida
Country Roads of Hawaii
Country Roads of Illinois, second edition
Country Roads of Indiana
Country Roads of Kentucky
Country Roads of the Maritimes
Country Roads of Massachusetts
Country Roads of Michigan, second edition
Country Roads of New Jersey
Country Roads of New Hampshire
Country Roads of New York
Country Days In New York City
Country Roads of North Carolina
Country Roads of Ohio
Country Roads of Ontario
Country Roads of Oregon
Country Roads of Pennsylvania
Country Roads of Tennessee
Country Roads of Vermont
Country Roads of Virginia
Country Roads of Washington

All books are $9.95 at bookstores.
Or order directly from the publisher (add $3.00
shipping & handling for direct orders):
Country Roads Press
P.O. Box 286
Castine, Maine 04421
Toll-free phone number: **800-729-9179**